Dedication

To everyone who has decided to break free from gutkha, smoking, or alcohol addiction—and to those who never fell into its trap.

ENOUGH I AM DONE WITH IT

• ALCOHOL • CIGARETTE • GUTKHA

HOW I HIT MY 'FACTORY RESET BUTTON' TO BREAK FREE

BIPIN

ISBN
Paperback 979-8-89929-866-0
Hardcase 979-8-89929-985-8

Contents

Disclaimer.. 11

Acknowledgement 13

About the Author 15

Prelude.. 17

Part One

The Texture of Addiction 23

The Feel 24

The Voice.. 33

The Theatrics 40

The Looks 46

The Fuel..52

The Emotions 58

The Influencers 63

The Exoticism 68

Part Two

When it starts hurting the most.....................................75

The Feel – Not Anaesthetic Any More 77

The Voice – Deafening...81

The Looks – Deceptive 84

Fuel – Values 87

Values mean nothing without action. 88

The Emotions – Scripted 90

The Dilemma – Unending 94

Part Three

The Verdict 99

Enough is Enough..101

Go Beyond your 'WHY' 106

The Preparation

If You Fall Back, Rise Stronger................................115

Show Vulnerability, Seek Help..................................122

Practice Mindfulness 129

The Triggers

Internal Triggers 139

External Triggers..146

Just One Last Time (The Myth) 152

Reinventing Yourself

Handling the Boredom After Quitting............................161

Cutting the Emotional Chord 174

Breaking the Subconscious Connection............................180

Trust Yourself...189

Celebrate Small Wins...194

Be Prepared – The World Doesn't Care About
Your Quitting..198

Visualise the Future...203

Forgiveness and Gratitude 207

Disrupt Your Own Narrative About Addictions.................212

Let the New Narrative Sink In...............................215

When you are ready, it's your turn..........................218

Part Four

Workbook..223

How This Workbook Is Structured.............................224

Workbook Part 1

Dig Deeper 226

Vulnerability is my strength. I respect that................237

■ Contents ■

My thoughts can't escape the radar. 242

I can handle triggers. 247

I accept myself the way I am...252

I am grateful...256

Forgiveness...260

Workbook Part 2

The Author's Personal Daily List – 1

(First 30 Days) 264

The Author's Personal Daily List – 2 269

Workbook Part 3

Break the Glass in Case of Emergency 274

Disclaimer

This book is a blend of personal reflection and narrative storytelling. While based on many real experiences, certain events, conversations, and details have been modified or fictionalized for narrative flow and context. The goal is to convey the emotional and psychological aspects of addiction and recovery rather than provide a literal account.

Any resemblance to actual persons, living or dead, is purely coincidental.

Quitting gutkha, smoking, or alcohol can have physical, psychological, and emotional effects. Readers are strongly advised to seek professional medical guidance before making the decision to quit.

The stories, perspectives, quotes, and references in this book are meant for motivational and inspirational purposes only. They should not be taken as medical, psychological, or professional advice. The author does not claim to provide definitive truths or prescriptive guidance but aims to encourage self-reflection and alternative viewpoints.

This book is not intended to defame any individual, organization, or entity. Readers are encouraged to interpret and adapt the content based on their own experiences. The publisher and author do not provide professional advice on the book's subject, and readers are solely responsible for their choices and decisions.

Language & Content Warning

The language in parts of this book is strong, raw, and blunt. Some expressions may be considered crude or indecent by certain readers. The intent is not to offend, but to provide an honest, unfiltered narrative.

Additionally, the book is about mature themes, including addiction and recovery, which may not be suitable for all readers.

If you're looking for polished or refined language, this may not be the book for you.

Given the subject matter, this book is intended for mature, adult readers only.

Acknowledgement

I am grateful to everyone who helped, encouraged, guided, and even pushed me to quit addictions—because at one point, it felt impossible. But here I am, sharing my story in the hope of inspiring others. If even one person finds the strength to quit, my gratitude to those who helped me will only grow stronger.

About the Author

Beyond addiction, **Bipin** writes about leadership, coaching, and the role of emotions in both personal and professional growth. His books include *Fostering Teams That Create Disruption*, *Vulnerability Intelligence*, and *Clearance Sale of Emotions*.

He believes in real conversations—the kind that challenge perspectives and inspire a real change.

With over two decades of leadership experience in the BFSI industry, Bipin brings a practical, human-first lens to his work. He lives in Pune, India, with his wife and two daughters.

To know more, you can visit his LinkedIn Profile.

https://www.linkedin.com/in/bgx/

Prelude

If you are holding this book, I know one thing—you are curious. Maybe you are curious about addiction itself, curious about why so many people fall into it, or about how to break free.

Let me be honest. Gutkha, cigarettes, and alcohol have become part of our culture.

We see it all around us, embedded in our definitions of celebration, love, unwinding, grieving and even ways to beat stress. It's like this -

Marriage invitation? "When's the cocktail night?"

Corporate party? "No alcohol? Are you kidding?"

Traveling abroad? "Pick up a few extra bottles from duty-free."

Gutkha? Exaggerating Ads.

Cigars? Wow, that Actor looks like a stud, a macho dude with a cigar in mouth.

I don't care why these products exist in the market.

What I do care about are the people—lying in hospital beds, struggling in rehab, burning their savings on addiction while their families suffer.

I probably can't change society. But if sharing my story—what helped me and what didn't. If it makes a difference for even one person, I would have done my part.

The irony that scares me the most is when people say:

"I don't see people dying from tobacco or alcohol. So, why should I quit?"

That's what I call an optical delusion.

But the question remains, why don't we see addiction-related deaths?

Here's my perspective:

We attend maybe 50–75 funerals in our lifetime, mostly of close ones. But how often do we actually see someone die of lung cancer, heart disease, or alcohol-related failure? Even when it happens, the cause is hardly linked to addiction.

But the truth is:

Tobacco kills nearly 8 million people every year.

Alcohol kills 2.6 million people annually.

Sources: WHO

I don't want to scare you or anyone with these reports, but I also do not want to sugarcoat the reality of addiction.

A little about me – I grew up in a city known for two things—its great historical heritage and its Gutkha culture.

Like many, my journey with addiction started out of curiosity.

At one point, I was having all, Gutkha, Cigarette, and Alcohol. But I never called myself an addict—because I didn't *want* to.

Eventually, as the pain of these substances kept on growing beyond my ability to handle them, I quit them.

When I said, 'Enough. I am done with it,' I quit them one by one—most of it, surprisingly easily.

I've shared most of that journey in this book.

And, I am incredibly thankful that you've picked up this book—whatever may be your reason. As you read, take your time. There's no rush. If you're looking to quit, do it because *YOU* want to.

And my story may not be yours, and vice versa. If you are looking to quit addiction, you might even do it faster than I did.

If this book helps you break free, I would love to hear your story.

A final word – If you're looking to quit, avoid moving directly to the 'how-to' part in the book. Go chapter by chapter. There's something in each one that might just change the way you see addiction.

Also, just to clarify—while I have focused on gutkha, smoking, and alcohol and sometimes referred to them collectively as "addiction" or "substance," I am actually referring to these three.

Also, just so you know—the tone and references in this book are shaped for someone who is looking to break free from addictions.

My best wishes.

Part One

The Texture of Addiction

Addiction doesn't just have a taste or a smell.

It has a texture, too.

I have touched it.

It feels like something.

It feels like the way it scripts your emotions, messes with your health, fogs your decisions, and distorts your sense of what's right.

And it's different for everyone.

And just like texture, it changes its colour over time.

What once felt fresh and thrilling, with time, feels stale and heavy.

This part of the book is about that feeling.

The feel of addiction when no one's watching.

The truth beneath the truth.

So run your hand across it and feel what's real.

And once you sense it, you can stop touching it.

To Call it quits.

The Feel

Meet Aryan.

A young marketing professional in Delhi.

Smart.

Opinionated.

And, couldn't work under pressure.

One evening, after a rough day—an argument with a colleague still stuck on replay—he walked into his usual bar-restaurant in Karol Bagh.

It was his after-office zone. A stop before heading home to tell his wife the final lie of the day as he would get late again - *"I had back-to-back meetings today, they suck more than they pay, I am completely drained out. Going to sleep"*

This was the place where his mind did the buffering to decide who was the 'biggest asshole' for the day.

And for now, the drinks hit just right.

Felt like money well spent.

That colleague? That argument? Gone from his mind.

Thanks, whisky.

He finished the last drink. But again, the winner of the title 'asshole for the day', that colleague, showed up in his mind.

He ordered one more.

'Just one last drink', he told himself. Likely the second last lie for the day.

Because he ordered one more.

He paid the bill and walked to the parking lot. As the early monsoon soaked the city, Aryan stepped into the rain and headed to his prized possession—a brand-new car.

He started driving. Turned on the AC. Played his favourite old songs.

Felt the bliss as everything looked euphoric.

The rain blurred the streetlights.

And a truck appeared out of nowhere. Suddenly.

"Shit!"

He hit the brakes.

Skid.

Inertia.

Bang. Boom. Crash.

Silence.

Next thing he remembers—

A voice. Inaudible almost.

"Sir? Sir, can you hear me?"

Pain. Red on his shirt. Cracked dashboard.

"You're lucky someone called for help; you could have died."

He woke up in the hospital emergency ward. The smell of antiseptic and medicine was the first to hit his senses. Pain in the forehead and chest. He didn't feel right in the ribcage.

"You hit a truck," the nurse said. "Loaded with iron bars. Your car's gone. You're alive. Are you drunk?"

Aryan did not make any eye contact and looked at his white shirt; it was red with his own blood.

Within less than two hours of binge drinking, his euphoria was already a nightmare. He was trying to connect the dots about everything.

Who was responsible? Who? Who?

The truck?

The rains?

That colleague?

The narrow roads?

The street lights?

Or all of them.

He himself was not an option to be responsible for it; because he was the victim.

He was hospitalised for almost ten days before he could join back to work with his head bandaged and a shoulder sling.

What happened? a colleague asked.

"Nothing? A truck came from the wrong side and banged my car; the driver was drunk," Aryan replied. "I have made a police complaint. It will get him to jail. We should drive safely; the roads are not safe."

* * *

Almost around the same time, somewhere else in Kolkata, Rahul, a college student, had his own trip of life when it came to addictions.

He wasn't into alcohol.

His thing was Gutkha: betel nuts mixed with tobacco, which made people look ugly and rich—rich if you carried boxes of branded Pan masala (betel nuts) and tobacco box in your hands.

Economy class, if you stuffed Gutkha in your pockets.

But the truth is most travel economy, like I did.

Rahul was also in the Student Union. And Gutkha in his mouth?

It fed his delusion

That it added to his persona—

In student politics,

Of a rebel brave heart

Of someone who had a *style* when he spat in the corners.

He started eating it during school when his uncle gave him some as he showed curiosity.

By the time he hit college, he was taking 15 sachets a day.

And believe me, he still falls in the amateur category because it comes to one gutkha per hour. Only.

What a shame.

And now, as his stained teeth exposed his habits, he didn't have to tell anyone that he was a gutkha guy.

His mouth was full of ulcers, and he could no longer eat whatever he wanted. But there was a perk of having loyal friends like his.

They could easily understand what he was saying with gutkha in his mouth, using the community language of Gutkha guys.

Which goes like 'Aww waa aw waa aa.'"

If you didn't get that, good for you. But I did because I was once a Great gutkha guy.

He said, 'I need to pee.'

But, you might be surprised, he had a girlfriend.

Well, I don't find it an aberration.

Do you know why? Because his girlfriend didn't have a choice, as most boys in the college were into this habit and had stained teeth. And she had to go 'Minmax' way.

Now, Rahul, with a decade of experience in Gutkha, could even sleep with one in his mouth.

And one day, when he was brushing his teeth in the morning,

One strike from the toothbrush burst an ulcer and left a wound that showed on the outside of his cheek.

"What the fuck" he said, looking himself in the mirror.

He got shit scared for the first time and rushed to the hospital. The doctor wasn't as shocked as Rahul was.

"We need to do a test for cancer," the doctor said, prescribing painkillers and other medicines and, of course, admitted him to the hospital.

* * *

And now, Meet Vishal.

An MBA student in Mumbai. A budding smoker. A gymmer and a self-proclaimed health freak.

He felt cigarette was a ritual, not a drug.

And smoked one before class. One after. One while thinking.

Twenty a day. Just.

He shared a rented room with a friend.

One evening, his roommate's girlfriend's parents came over to visit.

Vishal played a well behaved roommate. Sat on the side.

And then—

TA-DA.

His steel glass ashtray, hidden under the cot, tipped over.

Cigarette butts scattered everywhere.

Seventy. Maybe more.

Later, after the guest of honour went away, his roommate told him,

"Her dad said something downstairs."

"What? He didn't like you?," Vishal asked jokingly.

"He said that I was not in the right company."

He meant Vishal.

Vishal laughed. Lit another cigarette.

Didn't feel like an insult.

Just felt like life.

'And, what do you think good boy?' He asked.

Gentlemen, you might hate all three characters—Aryan, Rahul, and Vishal. But the truth is, once upon a time, I was just like them. Maybe even worse.

And for the same reason, I don't blame them for the addictions.

I feel bad for them; I feel sorry for them.

Maybe, deep down, they also want to quit.

Maybe they don't know how to quit. Maybe they tried and failed many times.

Or, maybe they are not yet ready to say, "Enough. I'm done with it."

Not Yet.

Why did I have to lose so much before I finally said, 'Enough is enough'?

The Voice

Let me start with another story. Just give me your attention for a minute.

Peter, a hunk was surfing in the Arabian sea. It was a sunny day. He moved with the waves—confident, flowing, almost poetically.

Then, out of nowhere, the sea changed.

A monster wave rose and crashed onto him, pulling him under.

He fought.

His lungs expanded.

His heart beat like - thum thum dub thum thum dub.

Even his gym-trained muscular body failed.

Seconds felt like hours.

Now, what do you think Peter could be craving in that moment?

If you said air—think again.

Peter wasn't craving oxygen.

He was craving life.

Addiction is the same.

You think you crave a cigarette.

Or a drink.

Or gutkha.

But what you're really craving is relief.

Distraction.

Control. Authority.

A sense of feeling ALIVE.

I am talking about things legally available in most parts of the world.

Take Aryan—our boy from Delhi.

The one who nearly died in an accident.

Who, someday started with a drink that made him so tipsy—something six pegs can't do today.

Why did he continue?

Because he handled cravings in his own way.

Strategically. Silently.

He never let cravings get loud.

He never found the eject button—the one that could give him a parachute to land safely.

Maybe he thought he didn't need one.

But that button was always there.

He could have pressed it after any sip, drag, or gutkha—and made it his last.

He just had to decide - This is the last one.

And press it.

But, in his mind, he wasn't addicted.

He was just going through some shitty phase of life. Almost every day.

Tough circumstances.

A dilemma that no one could understand.

But yes, he believed that when life got better, he'd quit.

Till then, he was so grateful that in tough times, at least alcohol was there for him.

Because, he believed that 'tough times don't last, but a man with alcohol does.'

I laughed while writing such a screwed-up belief. Not kidding. It made me nostalgic.

I mean it

One day, the universe, or maybe God wanted people with addictions to hear something in the silence of cravings.

So, COVID-19 appeared.

Shops shut.

No alcohol.

Nothing.

Can you believe that a few even drank sanitiser—because it had alcohol.

May God bless their souls on a serious note.

Some felt pain of cravings in the bones.

Some imagined that torture more painful than the 'third degree' in the Jail.

But Many, in those moments found out—they could survive days without it.

But unfortunately, our friends Aryan, Rahul and Vishal had to face the music as the cravings hit them silently.

Vishal, the hostel guy, stocked up on bidi bundles—along with whatever cigarette brand he could get his hands on. He hoarded as many as he could.

The truth is that we Don't Crave, We Just Get Trapped

I'm not a doctor. I'm not a scientist.

I don't understand dopamine or chemical dependency stats. While they could be important, but no one quits because of a fact or a data.

I hated when people said, "Are you craving a cigarette badly?"

It sounded like an insult.

I wasn't craving. I was running a well-defined process.

And every Addiction Has Its Own process.

Tobacco? That's the quick hit.

Always there. A little pack in your pocket, a quick reach, a flick of a lighter, and you're into it.

You don't even think. Muscle memory does it for you.

Alcohol?

It waits for you.

It's not a quick hit—unless you make it 90ml, neat, early.

It's a ritual.

The right time.

The right glass.

The first sip.

And Through It All, I kept Lying to Myself

I am in control because I don't drink every day,

But there were days when My Body Tried to Speak Up for my soul.

Some nights, I would wake up drenched in sweat.

Heart beating fast. Anxious for no reason.

Maybe it was the alcohol.

Maybe it was the stress.

Maybe it was something else.

The Blood pressure shot up.

The doctor doubled my meds.

ECG showed the first signs of heart problems.

A diastolic dysfunction—whatever the hell that meant.

And what did I do?

Did I stop drinking? Cut back?

No Sir.

I just avoided people who told me that.

To cut down.

The only question left was how much I was willing to lose,

to those silent cravings that had no voice?

Do we really have to hit the rock bottom before we hit the 'Reset button'?

The Theatrics

Where There Is Will, There Is Never a Way

Yes, you read that right. Because that's the theatrics of addictions.

And if that makes sense to you—well, I wish I had met you earlier. Maybe then, I wouldn't have spent years banging my head against the wall, thinking willpower was the answer.

People, mostly parents and well-wishers told our three boys about willpower.

"Be strong."

"Have some self-control."

Sounds great. Logical even. But let me tell you the people who advised them about will power were wrong as they do not know about addictions.

If quitting was just about "being strong," wouldn't more people have quit it by now?

And that's my point.

Because addiction doesn't give a damn about logic. It doesn't care how badly you "want" to quit. You can swear off cigarettes, alcohol, gutkha—whatever—only to come back to them.

If willpower worked, weight loss wouldn't be a billion-dollar industry.

Willpower certainly helps in delaying an immediate gratification, that's it. And, when it comes to substances. If fails.

Rahul, the gutkha guy, tried to quit using willpower.

To add some synergy, he teamed up with his elder brother—also into gutkha.

A senior, more seasoned addict. More years. More stains on the teeth.

They made a pact.

Quit together.

And to add some emotional fuel to their willpower, they swore on each other's lives.

"If we touch it again, the other one dies."

Sounds dramatic.

Because it is.

Funny? Hilarious? Yes.

But also—dead serious.

It worked for two day.

And then, they had a little heart-to-heart.

"You know, technically no one dies if you break a promise."

So, the treaty was broken.

Fighting Addiction Feels Like Fighting 'Bali' from Ramayan

Bali had this boon from God—whenever he fought someone, he got half of their strength. This made him invincible.

So, the stronger his opponent, the stronger he became. And the weaker they got.

My addiction worked exactly the same way.

Every time I fought it, it only got stronger.

My motivation? Cut in half.

My resolve? Weaker by half.

The moment I said, *"That's it, I'm quitting,"* the cravings hit twice as hard.

And every single time, I lost.

Here's what I finally realized:

Quitting isn't about willpower.

That's exactly why Aryan and Vishal also kept failing.

They went the wrong way.

Because addiction, like a Trojan had already rewritten their internal software.

The system that was supposed to detect and handle attacks?

Corrupted.

They believed willpower would work.

But it was never the antivirus they needed.

It was the wrong antidote.

What they needed wasn't complex.

It was simple. Direct. A clean swipe.

The kind of thing that looks the Trojan in the eye and says—*Fuck off. Types.*

Simple bro. That simple.

We all would have read and believed that our subconscious mind is many times more powerful than the conscious mind. At least, I believe now.

Our conscious mind works hard.

But the subconscious? That runs on autopilot.

That's why I kept falling back into the same patterns, no matter how much I wanted to quit. Willpower is part of the conscious mind.

While addiction was now part of the subconscious.

So, the real question was not about "being strong."

The real question was —how do I rewire the subconscious?

Because till I didn't?

I kept trying.

I kept failing.

When it comes to quitting alcohol or tobacco, is willpower really about power?

The Looks

"What's your poison today?"

It sounds like a sexy, attention-seeking one liner from a movie, doesn't it?

At least, to me, it did.

Some lines stick not because they're wise but because they seduce you.

The first time someone said this to me at a party, I added it to my dictionary.

I even started using it at my parties—feeling like some opulent host, playing bartender in my own film.

All this drama—because alcohol and tobacco are either glorified or romanticised.

The expensive brands are sold as symbols of status.

Success.

Even masculinity.

Or worse—positioned like a tranquilliser that can take your pain away.

But once the alcohol leaves your body, you realise that the pain's still there.

So, you go back to it.

Again.

And again.

Until the loop doesn't look like one. It becomes a part of life.

I knew smoking doesn't just kill.

It torments.

Not just the body—but the soul.

We've all seen those rotting lungs on cigarette packs.

We see them.

And still, we light up as if our lungs are immune to everything.

I'm sorry, it stings, sure.

Because it's better to sting now than too late.

Somewhere deep inside, a part of me, feeling ignored and tired

was Gaping at me, eyes wide open.

And at that moment, the choice was mine: to pay attention or to ignore it.

I once saw a movie scene set in a mental hospital. They made it funny—the actors playing the patients laughed at nothing, spoke gibberish, and reacted irrationally. The audience was supposed to laugh, too.

But then I thought—

Isn't that what drunk people look like?

Laughing at absurd things. Slurring. Doing things that wouldn't make sense to anyone except them.

And the best part? Most of them won't even remember it the next morning.

The sad difference?

One is considered illness. The other is celebrated.

The truth is that when chaos looks like a celebration, who questions it?

That's how invisible the real damage is. We don't see it.

Addiction turns people into versions of themselves that are not in control—we laugh it off, but it could actually be distressing.

One day, I saw just how brutal an addiction could be.

Incidentally, by then, I had already quit.

I was at a hospital, sitting in the waiting room. My cousin was undergoing surgery for mouth cancer—a result of years of gutkha.

He was a gutkha guy—not occasionally. Daily. Multiple times.

Now?

He has no cheeks left.

Part of his mouth is gone.

And for what?

A habit that gave him a five-minute high but took his flesh forever?

I felt sorry.

Sorry for him.

Sorry for every person lying in those cancer hospital beds…

Imagine there is this shopkeeper who sells products by saying:

"Buy this—it'll make your teeth yellow and rot your gums."

"Buy this—it'll burn your liver and damage your lungs."

"Buy this—it gives you a heart attack."

Who would buy that?

He is actually selling pain.

But if he sells it saying:

"This will give you joy and energy."

"This will multiply your celebrations."

"This will make you look alluring and get a fan club too."

People would line up to buy his stuff.

Because now, he's selling pleasure.

People would overlook pains.

And that's what makes the pain linked with addiction look invisible. Likely my cousin couldn't see the invisible too.

Because the looks are deceptive… and then, with time, you don't even care about the looks.

And the day we see that it is all about pain, feel that pain deep inside, we say

'Enough, I am done with it'

Because once you see it, you can't unsee it.

I don't blame myself because it took me time, but once I did, I realised it was all delusion.

The good news?

It took me nothing to fix that—just a change in perspective.

It meant confronting the pain I had been avoiding.

Yes, I had to feel some pain because for too long I had mistaken it for pleasure.

But it was worth everything.

Now, I know better. I know that looks can be deceptive.

For sure.

I didn't need profound wisdom to quit—just a bit of common sense.

That's my story in one line.

The Fuel

Our friends Aryan, Rahul, and Vishal tried quitting and met a therapist who

asked them to be mindful of the triggers that pulled them back toward the substance.

All three were surprised to realise that everything was a trigger.

Believe me, they were shocked.

Let me give you a taste of what they found:

Meeting friends? Tring.

Sitting in the car to drive? Tring.

Tired? Tring.

Thinking? Tring.

Holidays? Tring.

Sex? Tring, Tring, Tring.

Wife away? Tring.

Happy? Tring.

Old memories? Tring.

Just past the usual shop? Tring.

Someone said something? Tring.

You might get bored if I keep writing all of them.

But how the fuck is someone supposed to handle all those trings?

That's precisely what the boys asked their therapist.

If my current version was their therapist, I would've told them:

"Imagine you are in a bomb squad. Not just any squad— the best in the country. The nation needs you.

Now, when you hear those things, you're not supposed to handle all of them at once. You have to be mindful of them.

Just observe them. Identify them. And then, one by one... you defuse them."

Triggers are trespassers.

They travel with you—even if you change cities, jobs, or phones.

Let me ask you a wild question...

What if you were suddenly teleported to another planet?

A place where no one drinks, no one smokes.

No Gutkha. No Pubs. No nothing.

Just calm, clean, alien life.

What would happen?

My best guess? And, don't be surprised how sneaky the triggers can become.

Those aliens—those innocent, non-smoking folks—would become the trigger after a few days.

Because every time you see them, you'll remember you're the only one on the planet who is missing something.

The missing becomes the trigger.

The absence becomes the craving.

Having said that, when you don't feed a trigger, it slowly begins to lose its teeth.

And over time, it gets quiet.

It gets defused.

Triggers aren't about what you see.

They're about how you see.

All those things—shops, bars, gutkha packets, cigarette stalls—they already existed.

But we didn't see them as triggers until we linked them with addictions and emotions.

The addiction didn't start on Day One.

Do you remember your first smoke, drag, gutkha, or peg?

Most of them tasted awful.

At least to me, they did.

But as we connected them with joy, escape, and relief… they stopped being awful.

And slowly, we built our own triggers.

So, the way back is the same.

Defuse the triggers.

Unpack the emotions.

It's not as complicated as it might feel.

Sometimes, noticing a trigger is the start of changing it.

Now, did you notice something?

We started this chapter by calling *triggers* *as* **fuel for addictions**.

It felt something heavy. Loaded. Something no one can escape.

But then, as we moved forward, we started calling it a **"Tring."**

It suddenly didn't seem so terrifying, did it?

Like the sound of a phone. Something playful.

We reframed it. Still there. But not something huge.

Instead, it gives you the choice to pick that phone.

You can let it ring.

You can even smile at it.

You can say, "I am busy" And then keep walking.

And the more you let the 'tring' ring without answering, the quieter it becomes.

I'll share more about handling triggers later in the book because I'm committed to giving you enough to break free.

And if it works for you, please do let others know how you did it.

I kept trying to fix the external triggers for my addictions—until a wise man told me to look within.

The Emotions

The reality is that when someone tries to talk about the emotions embedded with alcohol or tobacco, very few understand.

Like if I scream in front of a few people, "I am screwed"

Everyone will get what I am going through.

'I am in deep trouble.'

It's as simple as that.

But when Aryan screams, "I need a drink" no one really gets it—except another person who drinks too.

Only the ones who are into that addiction would understand it.

They would feel for Aryan while others wouldn't.

They would know he needs it now—and that it's the most important and the most urgent thing for him.

And if addiction could speak?

Or, if it could write to our boys Aryan, Rahul, and Vishal a love letter. It would be something like -

My Love,

I always knew you would find me.

I had been waiting patiently, quietly. Why did you take so long? I knew you'd get here finally. They all do.

And once you found me, I have always been here for you, haven't I? Through your screwups and your wins. I never judged you like others, never asked questions. I just made your life easy to handle.

You came for me, and I held you. You needed a break, and I was there.

People tell you that you are addicted to me. They are so wrong. Because love is not an addiction.

Remember the first time? You chose me. We liked each other.

And then you took me to all weddings, parties, and late nights—I was always invited. You refused to go without me.

And when you thought about leaving me, I opened the doors to make a way.

But you never could.

Maybe you need me more than I need you.

This is love, sweetheart—not addiction.

Even if you are unwell, you still reach for me.

When I take away your sleep, your health, your money— you still take my side and ready to fight the whole world.

And, you know, the way you turn the bottle upside down before drinking and pat it as a ritual to loosen the cap,

The way you caringly cover the flame that lights up the cigarette,

And even the way you lovingly tear open the Gutkha sachet.

It feels so much like foreplay.

That's love, isn't it?

You can pretend to fight me.

But we both know—I live in you now.

I know your cravings before you do.

I know your triggers, your likes and dislikes.

Because I am you now.

Love, Always.

Gutkha, Cigarette, Alcohol.

There is a hidden agenda of addictions in that loaded love letter,

Even our three boys, Aryan, Rahul, and Vishal—they had to live with it until the day they could finally read between the line.

How emotions change? let me share more.

I was a teenager when we had a wedding in the family. Back then, the excitement was real.

Meeting cousins I hadn't seen in ages.

Staying up late just to watch the rituals.

The celebrations felt endless.

It was pure and unwinding with no complications. Just being there was the thing.

And, Fast forward a few years.

Another wedding. My priorities had changed.

It wasn't about the people, the ritual, or the celebration anymore.

It was about finding out something.

Which fucker was organising the bottles for those 'before dance' quick shots?

Which room?

Which car boot?

The actual wedding felt like a byproduct.

The real ritual was making sure that my Whisky found me.

And if it didn't?

Screw the wedding.

I wasn't celebrating—I was enduring.

Let me get serious about emotions and addiction.

No one can take away our emotions.

They are like muscles hiding behind fat.

It's said that we all have six-pack abs - just covered.

Same with emotions.

They get layered and repackaged.

Addiction doesn't erase pain or fear - it hides them behind manufactured joy and bloated confidence.

But it never wipes out the real stuff - joy, grief, excitement, sadness.

Why?

Because it can't.

The addiction doesn't remove pain.

No Sir, it doesn't.

Even anaesthesia wears off—and the pain comes back.

And that's the point.

The Influencers

Aryan and a few colleagues at an office party were laughing loudly at a pub. As usual, they were celebrating nothing in particular - just bitching about their bosses and teasing a colleague who, that very morning, had gotten screwed by the president for some fuckup.

They were all three or four pegs down—except Ronit.

The new joinee.

A teetotaler.

Just trying to blend in.

He sat there quietly, feeling out of place.

He hated alcohol.

Because he'd seen what it could do.

His father died because of it.

Feeling restless, he leaned in and asked one of his colleagues.

"Do you know what's written on the whisky bottle?"

"No, I don't," the guy replied amusedly and continued.

" Aryan, tell HR to check whether the candidate drinks or not during the interview—and only hire those who do"

Everyone erupted in drunken laughter. Ronit smiled faintly.

Aryan barged in, already slurring a bit.

"It's written—'Alcohol is injurious to health'—just like *you* are to our fun!"

Again, they all laughed.

Ronit still didn't give up. He smiled wryly and said:

"Those warnings aren't there because someone cares for you.

They're there so that when addiction kills you, you only have yourself to blame.

It's on you. You chose death."

For a second, the laughter stopped.

People looked at each other like bloody hell, maybe it was time to get serious.

And suddenly, someone made a funny sound—

and everyone started laughing, louder this time. Howling madly.

While you might relate to such conversations, one thing's clear—

Everyone who drinks or chews tobacco or smokes already knows the truth.

It's no secret.

Even a child knows these things are harmful.

So, there has to be something powerful—like a magnetic field that influences moving charges to create electricity. It's hard to escape its presence

But, having escaped three times, let me share my perspectives.

It might sound dramatic, but I mean it—Triggers, as discussed earlier, are the hunters that haunt you—till they can matter to you.

And influencers?

They are like undertakers.

The ones who fix that moment,

Push you toward the fall,

While you're still trying to figure out—

Why am I liking this fall?

Let me add to it: a hoarding with a Gutkha ad or a song with the word 'whisky', a surrogate ad that reminds one of a liquor brand, or even a movie scene showing the actor holding a cigar and looking larger-than-life—all of these triggers might create cravings.

But again, the influencers?

You just need to be there with the people who make it feel normal.

The one who laughs a little louder after every peg.

The one who strikes a pose—chin up, eyes half-closed, every time they pull a drag.

And surprisingly, if you don't drink?

They ask questions, just like in Ronit's case.

"No drink at all?"

"Who hired you?"

What a sick comment to make.

And

Once you are into addiction, you, too, become part of influencers.

Unknowingly.

Subtly.

And that's the irony of addictions.

Shared lighters, shared emotions, shared silences, and a promise to support each other only till everyone is tipsy.

Having said that, I don't know much about drugs.

But people who are into them?

Even in a new city, they somehow figure it out.

No ads. No boards. No Google search. Just looks. Just people.

That's scary.

That's influence.

It's people. Always people.

The most dangerous influencers weren't hoardings or lyrics or surrogate ads.

They were people.

The ones who were showing off.

The ones who were looking for a fan club, followers or a tribe.

Even the closest ones—people who *knew* I was trying to quit—

would say with a mocking grin,

"Tumse nahi hoga. Stop that nautanki, … le, pakad glass."

(You can't do it. Stop the drama—and here, hold this glass.)

That's when I tried to connect the dots.

If addiction has so many influencers,

then who will influence me to quit?

Can you take a guess?

While you do your work, I will share how I handled those influencers, just in a while.

Till then, ruminate who your triggers and influencers are.

The Exoticism

Let me share about addiction from different lens. An interesting one.

'Foxy Exoticism'.

Have you seen the movie *Fifty First Dates*? A brilliant film.

The actress wakes up every morning, forgetting everything.

The actor must make her fall in love with him again every single day.

Is he able to do it?

You might have to watch the movie, I wouldn't tell.

But reminded me of how addiction behaved with me.

Because every time I swore to quit—gutkha, cigarettes, alcohol—and went to sleep with the highest resolve, the next evening…

I forgot what I had promised myself.

Memory loss? No.

Emotional seduction? Yes.

Addiction knew precisely how to win me over again.

But unlike any movie, this wasn't a love story that ended after a few hours.

This was life.

And that's not love.

That's Exoticism. Persistent. Desperate.

Our boys never threw away the leftover bottles, cigarettes, or gutkha when they quit.

"Why waste them?"

And when they relapsed?

That wisdom felt so fair.

All this because their emotional chord with foxy exoticism, the addiction stayed as it was.

I remember taking my five-year-old nephew often to the market.

He'd always ask for a chocolate.

His body changed the moment we reached the shop— eyes lit up, subtle joy on his face.

As the shopkeeper handed it to him, he looked at me with that grateful smile.

Was that addiction?

A need? or

Just a behaviour?

Let's sit with that for a second.

I think it was something else.

A link which led to joy.

Simple, pure joy.

But as he grew older, that link faded.

He found new sources of happiness and Joy.

He learned chocolate wasn't good for his teeth or tummy.

He moved on.

And that's the thing.

At times, you don't have to quit with a heavy heart.

You just have to make it… irrelevant.

Unneeded. Unimportant.

You have to outgrow it and break free.

Maybe you've crossed this bridge a hundred times in your head.

But maybe this time—you'll cross it for real.

And maybe this time, you won't look back.

Because that version of you—the one before addiction—

It is still there.

You don't need a perfect plan.

You just need to take the first step.

Like an umbrella that once covered me in the rain,

Addiction felt like my cover—

Protecting me from emotions I didn't want to handle,

Shielding me from a reality I feared to face.

But then one day,

I closed that umbrella…

And realised—

The rain was never real.

I was not covering myself.

I was hiding. Just hiding.

That… was my moment of truth.

And I quit.

Finally.

Part Two

When it starts hurting the most

When something just slightly bothers you, you brush it off.

Shrug. Move on.

But when it turns into a real pain in the ass—

You can't ignore it.

You want to fix it. *NOW.* Before anything else.

And then you realise,

You read it wrong.

That pain?

It's deeper.

Trickier.

Messier than you imagined.

And what makes it worse?

It's all happening in the mind.

The moment you ignored it and the moment it messed with you.

Both started in the same place.

The mind.

And now, it hurts even more.

Having been through it,

here's what I have to say:

You don't need to go through all this pain.

You can break free from it earlier.

Many do.

In the next few pages, let me share what could be happening underneath—

not in the body,

but in the heart and mind.

The emotions.

Stuck with a script.

Urge. Hope.

Maybe you'll find your own moment of:

"Enough. I'm done."

Maybe it's already beginning.

And even if you can't see the way out yet—

doesn't mean there isn't one.

The Feel - Not Anaesthetic Any More

It was sad when Aryan realised that his usual after-office stop at Karol Bagh was no longer just a chill break before home.

It had become a cost centre.

His rationale?

Why spend 1000/- for 4 pegs when I can buy a whole bottle with the same amount and drink at home?

My wife won't nag me for being late. Plus, I can save, maybe even upgrade to scotch. Crash straight onto the bed. No stress of driving. No trucks on the way.

Sounds brilliant, right?

What he didn't see was—this was not brilliant.

This was a trap, a slow sinking quicksand.

One he was setting up for himself.

And now, even the bottle wasn't working like before.

The arguments with his wife had turned near-violent.

The pleasure had changed into pain, even torture.

The whisky's not the problem. People are.

They are assholes.

All of them.

What once felt great was now felt like a pain.

The whisky that helped him crash fast now made him restless in the nights and drained in the mornings.

He started drinking when the sky was blue and passed out when it was black.

Woke up with the blues and a mind blacked out.

I too have lived that.

I have felt the same fatigue.

The same drained-out body.

The same messed up story.

You want to say, "Enough."

But something holds you back.

You judge people wrong, and that wrong feels right.

It may feel like driving in your nightmare and taking the wrong road.

The more you drive, the farther you go from your destination.

But You can stop.

You can take a U-turn.

Even if there is anger, guilt, and shame for reading the map wrong and choosing the wrong road.

But once you turn?

Things start getting clearer. Cleaner and sorted.

Believe me—

Taking that U-turn is as simple as it sounds.

And only you get to decide when you want to take the U-turn.

Vishal was smoking 40 cigarettes a day now. He had completed his MBA and had a corporate job. He was earning well enough, so he no longer smoked BIDIs or cheap brands.

He had upgraded to an expensive lighter and brand.

Even Cough had upgraded.

And his car?

It smelled like nicotine. He kept an air freshener for visitors, hiding the smell.

And, cigarettes had stopped giving him the pleasure they once did.

It wasn't about a style quotient anymore; it was about feeding his nerves with nicotine. Just a burden.

Even Rahul, who had a close escape from cancer, couldn't break free.

And don't we see often?

Even after heart surgery, people still can't quit alcohol.

Because the pain of not having it feels bigger than the pain they had with that heart attack.

His family was shocked—

"How can someone be this stupid?"

Maybe they were just simple people who didn't know how addiction messes up the brain.

All three of them wanted to press that reset button—

The one that erases all memories of addiction.

What they didn't know was—

That reset button?

It was already inside them.

Because deep down, they always knew these substances were wrong.

The addiction had just numbed that voice.

And now?

They could hear it again.

Loud. And clear. I can vouch for it.

The Voice - Deafening

What does a person do when they start sitting alone with their addiction?

Let's say alcohol.

Just them. And the bottle.

Most people I've seen don't start slow.

They hit fast-forward—the first peg is big, and the time to finish it is small. Go, went, gone.

Why?

Because they were missing that sting, that spark in the brain that zaps them back to the vibrations they need.

That voice in their head probably sends a signal to the throat—it starts squeezing.

Then it moves to the tongue—it starts craving.

Then the heart—it starts beating faster, shouting:

"Now, make it fast!"

It's not the heart talking.

It's not even the craving.

It's the addiction.

And the longer you ignore it, the louder it gets.

The first peg?

It's not for pleasure.

It's to shut that voice up.

You give in—not because you want it—

but because you **can't stand that noise.**

That's why most people prefer this ritual solo.

They don't want anyone else to hear that voice.

And it's not just alcohol.

Tobacco speaks, too.

More often. More persistently.

It doesn't scream. It pokes.

It taps on your nerves.

It makes you feel anxious with things that were never supposed to bother you.

A meeting. Traffic. Or any random situation.

But here comes the interesting part.

Because it has a voice—

you can choose not just to hear it but to listen.

And ask it some real questions:

"Why do I make the first one larger?"

Maybe more.

The truth is, we find it deafening because we keep listening to it.

But can we learn to ignore it?

Yes.

And we do—when we choose to.

Even the worst voice eventually goes mute—if you learn to answer back.

It is all about making your own voice bigger and saying—

"ENOUGH."

If addiction can yell this loud, imagine how powerful your 'Enough' could be.

The Looks - Deceptive

Poet Gertrude Stein once wrote:

"A rose is a rose is a rose."

She probably meant that no matter what you call a rose, it stays a rose.

A symbol of love. Beauty.

Let me be poetic too—maybe not as philosophical, but definitely more critical:

An addiction is an addiction is an addiction."

Call it a habit.

Call it a way to chill.

Call it a personal choice.

Call it a stress reward system.

It doesn't change a thing.

And yes—if feel that you are *just mildly addicted*—

this might sting more.

Especially when someone says these words out loud.

Or worse… when you read them and it still strikes a chord.

But the truth is—addiction has no levels.

It's like driving fast or slow toward a cliff's edge.

Either way, you're still going to fall.

It might sound preachy, but believe me—

When it starts to hurt more, the looks of addiction get even more deceptive.

The outcomes, the intake, the speed—everything starts to look acceptable.

But only to the one who's consuming it.

Everyone else sees the mess clearly.

And that's the point.

What does addiction look like?

Let's take alcohol.

To one, it looks like a way to accept the status quo.

To another, a way to stay in the victim story.

To someone else—fuel for messing with their own character.

Same thing. Different looks.

So deceptive. Disguised.

But once you spot the disguise, you can refuse to dance to its tune.

And once you do that, you break free.

Fuel - Values

It might sound bizarre—what do values have to do with Addiction?

Honestly? Everything.

On the surface, nothing seemed to change with Aryan, Rahul, or Vishal. They looked the same. Talked the same. Smiled the same.

But deep down? There was a shift.

Their values changed.

From health to indulgence.

From connection to escape.

From care to *I don't care.*

They stopped caring about turning people into passive smokers. About the trash they left behind—gutka pouches, cigarette butts, that stale smell of alcohol in the room.

Between family time and drink time, they chose the latter.

Let me put it this way, Addiction hits people more vehemently who don't have a value system, like the ones who don't value time, health, peace, family, growth, love, and so many more things.

They fall quick prey to Addiction.

We can look around and see.

At the same time, people who value all these things would know the real face of substance.

But here's the universal truth:

Values mean nothing without action.

You can preach. Post quotes. Even write them down.

But if your actions don't match, they're just an illusion.

It reminded me of a woodcutter.

A man who lived by hard work and toiled with his axe every day. He valued discipline, effort, and sweat.

Then, one day, he stumbled upon a bag full of gold.

He didn't steal it. He didn't earn it. He just found it.

And that was enough to break him.

He stopped working. Got lazy. Spent the gold. Wasted it.

By the time the gold was gone, so were his values.

If Addiction and values could truly coexist, there wouldn't be signs on the roads that say *Don't drink and drive or Your family is waiting for you at home.*

Someone I know had a heated argument with his father after coming home drunk.

What a shame.

He came to me crying the next day—ashamed, sorry, and guilty.

I told him exactly this:

"The part of you that realises the mistake and feels guilty is also the part that's ready to change. So go home and say sorry from the heart. And show it in your behaviour, too."

Every time you choose your values, the Addiction starts losing its grip.

But until then, nothing really changes.

The Emotions - Scripted

Have you seen the award-winning movie *The Truman Show*?

It's one of those films that makes you question everything. I found it intelligent and touching at the same time.

At first, it seemed like a simple story. But as it went on, I thought—*What if this was me? Could this happen to me?*

My life had become almost similar.

Every action, every habit, every craving followed a pattern.

I knew exactly when and where to light a cigarette, which shop to go to, and how long until the next one.

It all felt natural—until one day, I started reading between the lines.

I believe you truly enjoy any movie when you let your emotions flow freely with the story.

We all know Superman or Spiderman will destroy the bad guys, but we still root for them.

We still feel the suspense, the tension, the hope, all along

That's how emotions work—they want to believe.

Why talk about people like Aryan, Rahul, or Vishal, who have their own stories?

Let me talk about myself.

In real life, when every emotion feels scripted, every action predictable you start hating it.

I didn't feel in control anymore.

I felt *controlled*. Damn restricted.

Maybe you are starting to feel it, too.

That illusion.

After a point, I wasn't even chasing the dragon. I was just following the drill.

I would sit in the mess, emotionally drained.

I knew the morning after—alcohol wouldn't feel the same. My mind wouldn't feel the same.

My body would not feel relaxed.

The next day would be punishment.

But still, when I sat again with the bottle—only "do not disturb me" mattered.

You stop caring about how you'll feel in the morning, or even tomorrow.

Sometimes, I wished someone—anyone—could give me advice.

Someone who really understood my inner self.

Let me ask a hypothetical question:

If you could meet your past and future selves face-to-face, who would give the best advice on quitting?

You'd probably say your future self.

But no. Not really.

It's your present self who knows what it looks like—the excuses, the cravings, the shame maybe.

Your present self knows the reality.

And here's the truth—people don't love their addictions. I never did.

I hated them. That's why I quit them, one by one.

When you're deep in it, you don't *love* that bottle, that cigarette, that gutkha.

You just co-exist. Maybe I'm repeating this thought. But it needs repeating.

You wake up, blame your boss, your spouse, the world.

And when there's no one left to blame—you blame yourself.

I know that. I bloody well know that.

When I feel angry, my heart beats faster. When I am afraid, my pupils dilate. When I'm low, my face drops.

Emotions lead how our body behaves.

And addiction? It messes with that.

It tricks the brain. But the body knows.

The body knows those emotions are fake.

Over time, the body learns—those feelings came *from* the substance.

So when you quit, your body *craves* those emotions. That's why withdrawal feels like an emotional mess.

Just before I made up my mind to quit, my emotions said:

I don't deserve this.

I can do better than that.

I'm setting the wrong example for my kids.

This adds nothing to my life.

But then, just a few days in, came the thought.

How would I live without it?

And that's how substances script your emotions.

Addiction distorts emotions. Reactions. Even our perception.

When you begin to see that crack, the reality of how your emotions were scripted, it means you're on the cusp.

Closer than you think to breaking free.

And believe me, you're not stuck.

You just need to push the door.

The Dilemma - Unending

I recall a dialogue that I'm not sure is from a movie or not. Full credit to its makers:

"Isko liquid oxygen mein daal do... Liquid isko jeene nahi dega, aur oxygen isko marne nahi dega."

(Put him in liquid oxygen... The liquid won't let him live, and the oxygen won't let him die.)

Sounds so resonating with -

The urge wouldn't let them quit.

Hope wouldn't let them give up.

Surprisingly, our boys—all three of them with different substances—were facing the same confusion.

It was:

Urge—for gutkha, smoking, alcohol.

Hope—that tomorrow would be the day I quit.

If you look closely, the urge is always for today.

Hope is always for tomorrow.

And that's why we tend to give the urge more attention.

At this point, their battle wasn't just about quitting.

It was about hating the urge itself.

People telling them to quit didn't matter anymore.

Their urge kept growing.

And the time between urges?

Kept reducing.

But hope?

Hope was reclamation.

Not just of their body—but of their soul too.

Hope was the light even a man buried beneath gravel could still see.

Hope was the belief that they could quit.

Wouldn't we agree that *if we still hope, even a little, it means we have not given up.*

So, keeping that hope alive was what they chose.

They were not just on the cusp of quitting addiction—but on the cusp of reclaiming themselves.

The Way Out – ENOUGH, I Am Done With It

Saying *Enough* doesn't always mean you've hit rock bottom.

Sometimes, it just means—you're done.

Done with something that doesn't feel right anymore.

Something that was never really *you*.

As simple as that.

One guy smoked just once or twice a day.

Another drank maybe once a month.

To the world, they looked like good boys and girls in the neighbourhood.

But addiction isn't about what others see. It's about how you see yourself.

When it feels like 'enough,' it comes from inside.

Like a verdict.

You stop explaining.

Stop pretending you're okay with it.

Now, you can clearly see the deceptive looks, hear the voice, and feel those scripted emotions.

And you just say it—

ENOUGH. I am done.

Aryan. Rahul. Vishal. Each hit that moment.

Maybe Not on the same day. Maybe Not in the same way.

But when it came—it was real.

They said *Enough is Enough.*

Like I did.

Like millions before you have done it.

And with that—half the battle is already won.

Part Three

The Verdict

Enough is Enough

Let me confess, even when I started writing this part of the book after sharing my experience with addictions, I felt damn relieved.

I wouldn't have to talk about the messy things now.

It already feels better.

Why?

Because earlier I had to replay those emotions in my mind.

Just like we still feel uneasy days after we recall an old nightmare in our minds.

And if you are reading this book to understand what worked for me and how it can help you break free from Gutkha, cigarettes, or alcohol.

You might have a question.

How the hell was this time different?

Just by saying enough is enough, is it?

What changed?

So here is my answer -

This time there was no Plan B.

No backup.

No, "just one last time."

No, "I'll quit tomorrow."

No "after this event" or "after whatever."

Not in my mind.

Not if I slipped.

Not even if someone gifted me complimentary bottles of 18-year-old vintage whiskey or a box of premium Cuban cigars that would've once made me weak and distracted.

This time, I wasn't fighting to quit.

I was just done with it.

In the next few pages, I have shared what things I did that helped.

I found that Quitting was not as difficult as I used to think.

In short.

Mornings were different now.

No more waking up to check if I had enough stock.

No more planning for the evenings.

Anyone who tried to stop me from quitting? They felt like the enemy.

Like roadblocks, be it my family members, friends or strangers.

I started planning my day.

I lived moment by moment.

Hour by hour.

I was as nimble-footed as the tightrope walker—you don't think about reaching the end; you just ensure that you keep walking without falling. No emotions or thoughts can pass through your head without your awareness.

But I won't lie. The cravings came.

They were strong.

But I was prepared.

Strong? I am not sure. But I was prepared.

And what did I do?

Imagine—what do you do when you see someone at a supermarket you don't want to talk to for any valid reason?

You don't make eye contact.

You don't engage.

You just keep moving, doing what you need to.

That's precisely what I did with cravings.

To begin with.

Now -

- Willpower? Not needed.

- Fighting it? Not needed.

- Blaming situations? Not needed.

All you need is clarity—and I'll share everything I've got.

Every trick.

Every failure.

Every lesson shared here was learned the hard way.

I hope this helps you immensely in what you seek.

Notes:

(Use this space to scribble anything that strikes a chord.

An idea, a plan, or even a feeling.

This space is yours)

I didn't have to quit an addiction—I had to grow beyond it.

Go Beyond your 'WHY'

Why, as in - Why do you want to quit that addiction?

Obvious reasons could be that you hate it, suffer because of it, or something else.

The reality about quitting an addiction is that most people who guide you to quit tobacco, alcohol, or any addiction tell you to first write down 100 reasons—your WHY for quitting.

They say, "Make a list. The longer your list is, the easier it gets."

But here's the truth—

Most of them have never been addicted themselves or might not have experienced what it takes to quit. The real WHYs.

They give advice that sounds right but does not actually work when you need something more than that.

However, a few of the common 100 'WHY' could be like:

- It's terrible for my health.

- My family suffers because of it.

- I waste 'x' money every month that I could use for my kids.

- I lose time and productivity.

- I lose control every time I have it.

- It causes fights at home; I just want peace.

- I feel guilty after every time I have it.

- I smell bad with it.

- It makes me look older than I am.

- It's embarrassing when my kids or family see me with it.

- I can't even enjoy social events without it.

- I get anxious and irritated when I don't have it.

- It's making me dependent—I don't feel normal without it.

- I've tried to quit so many times, and I feel like a failure.

- It's ruining my confidence.

- I wake up feeling awful every morning.

- I can't focus properly at work or on important things.

- It has messed up my relationships, even I have started avoiding people.

- I know I'm not in control of my own life because of addictions.

Now tell me—

How many times have you already thought about these things?

A hundred? A thousand?

And yet—you still didn't quit.

Because of those reasons.

They are real, but not enough.

They don't hit hard.

They are just the tip of the iceberg—the visible part.

The real reasons?

They live under the surface.

Let me share my WHYs candidly.

The Real Reasons that Supported Me to Quit

I didn't need 100 reasons.

I needed just a few—but they were burning from inside.

Here's what I wrote:

- I want to quit this gutter, filthy, stinking habit. I can't bloody stand it anymore.

- I am losing my ambition, my dream, because of this shit. This rotting shit.

- It makes me feel like a Big blooming loser.

- It doesn't help me in any way—NOTHING. Not even happiness. It just makes me insane.

- I don't deserve this shit because I have NO control over myself when I have it.

- My failures to quit till now have made me stronger and more informed. Now I know this stink, this bloody thing better. I know it in and out.

- My God, Hanuman Ji, is with me and gives me the power I need to quit. Every time I read these lines, I get even stronger.

And, every time I read these words, they increased my rigour even more than the one I had when I wrote them.

And if they didn't hit hard enough, I made them by adding verbs, adjectives, nouns, or whatever.

I made it as raw and real as I felt.

I wasn't writing a list to convince myself logically.

I was writing something that made me angry.

Something that made my heart beat faster.

Something that made me hate addiction to even touch, see or talk about.

Because quitting isn't just about listing WHYs—it's about finding the one that hits so deep, you can't ignore it anymore.

The one that makes quitting not a decision but the only option.

When your reasons are raw enough, ugly enough, and real enough, you won't need many to make a big list.

The point is that you need to find the smell of the WHY, like something that you cannot just stand.

You only need a few. The real ones.

The one that makes you say it—and never forget the moment you did: "I am Done with it."

The deeper, sharper, and more real your WHY, the easier it gets to quit.

Do whatever works for you.

Write down your reasons.

Carry them in your pocket.

Read them a few times a day, especially during the first month.

It helped me more than I thought.

In that list, you may choose not to write about any old bad experiences, but you may write about the emotions you felt at that time.

For me, the WHYs were slightly different for Gutkha, Smoking and alcohol, but the intensity was the same. For Gutkha, it was about feeling and looking ugly and Pathetic with stained teeth. For smoking, it was about 'being an idiot to get another tobacco addiction after quitting Gutkha' or about 'planning for my own shorter life'.

A spiritual person once told me that demons consume fire and smoke. That thought stuck with me—' smoking made me feel like an ugly demon.'

You might find it strange, but to me, it hit deep in the list.

Let me also share two things that I did.

Firstly, I chose my WHY from deep down, something that could be at the subconscious level and not a day-to-day thing.

Secondly, my WHY was very private, and I didn't share it with anyone. I did not write it on paper; I typed it on my mobile. But I am sharing my list with everyone now.

I never felt the need to put encouraging posters at home or anywhere. The list was enough.

Once you find your real WHY,

the hardest part is already done.

The rest will follow.

I believe we need to *write the WHYs down* before we move ahead.

And its ok if it takes a day or two to do this.

You will thank yourself later. Just do it.

Notes:

(Use this space to scribble anything that strikes a chord.

An idea, a plan, or even a feeling.

This space is yours)

The Preparation

If You Fall Back, Rise Stronger

It might feel demotivating to talk about falling back at this point. So early.

But trust me, the fear, the "what if," and the doubt—they might come too soon after we quit.

Even after writing down my strongest WHYs, I faced that fear, and that's ok.

The first two or three days felt surprisingly easy. But then—

Spark hums.

Muscle memory.

Emotional memory.

Time-of-day memory.

Everything came crawling back.

Day 2 to Day 8 After I Quit (Gutkha, Smoking, and Alcohol)

10 AM – Craving hit. I ignored it. Craving died.

10:30 AM – Craving hit back. I ignored it. Craving died again. Read my WHYs.

11 AM – Stronger craving. I felt softer. Read my WHYs.

1 PM – Craving surged. I felt weak but held on. Read my WHYs.

5 PM – Craving came with logic. I felt weak again. Read my WHYs.

9 PM – Craving returned. I was stronger.

Then it hit me again:

Saw a friend using it—craving.

Saw someone buying it—craving.

Felt angry—craving.

Same time of day—craving.

But I was ready.

I wasn't fighting it.

I was growing stronger.

Cravings will grow. That's not the problem.

They try to mess with your brain, patterns, emotions and habits.

But remember this—

Even breaking a simple habit takes effort.

And this is more than a simple habit.

Try this right now:

Clutch your hands together like you always do.

Notice which thumb sits on top.

Feels natural, right? That's your default.

Now—interlock your fingers the other way.

Put the other thumb on top.

Awkward? Uncomfortable?

Exactly.

That's what breaking a habit feels like in the beginning.

Not impossible. Just uncomfortable.

Keep doing it long enough.

Your new pattern becomes your new default.

That's how change begins with awareness and conscious efforts.

Imagine breaking something your body and mind have been addicted to for years.

It's not just a physical thing. It's emotional. Deep. Real.

And that's why we fall back.

Not because we're weak—

But because the new way feels wrong initially.

And the Cravings don't trap you by showing up.

They ambush you the moment you start paying attention to them.

One moment, you feel strong.

The next, you're telling yourself it's ok—

Just one more time.

So don't give it any attention.

Don't argue with it.

Don't try to convince it with rationale.

Don't reason with your own resolve.

And don't even curse it.

Instead—go back to that moment when you said, "ENOUGH."

Feel that emotion again. The anger. The disgust. The shame. The frustration.

Let it hit you—in your chest. In your guts

Feel it in your body. Let your body remember what it felt like to say "Enough."

Do it subtly. Quietly. But powerfully.

And yes, a doctor told me something important.

He said:

"Lapses happen."

And they did.

I lapsed twice when I tried quitting alcohol.

But here's what I learned—

I grew stronger after each lapse.

Every time I went back to the addiction, I hated it more than before.

I saw it for what it was.

And I quit again.

The trap isn't the lapse.

It's the thinking that you've failed.

But when you rise again?

You come back with more power.

More awareness.

More fire.

And let me say this—unlike me not everyone lapses or relapses.

Some people walk away and never look back.

Why Do People Fall Back?

- Too much free time.

- No healthy substitute.

- Carrying emotional baggage—anger, guilt, anxiety, self-pity.

- Thinking early "I am out of the woods."

What helped me?

I made a list of moments when I was steady, confident, and on top of things. I didn't just remember them—I relived them. I felt them in my breath, my body, and my posture.

Sometimes, what works for you is the only thing that matters.

To sum it up—

No one was born with addictions.

We've all quit things before.

This is no different.

When your body, mind, and soul align, quitting doesn't feel hard.

It feels natural. Even effortless.

But if you slip?

Go back.

Rewrite your WHY again.

Make it hit harder.

I added this line to my WHY list:

I fell back for it because I was not fully healed. But now—I see clearer. I feel stronger. I understand myself better. And I am DONE with it.

One confession:

Even though I felt upset about the lapse, I was more prepared.

More grounded.

More confident.

And I quit again, finally.

Like before.

Easily.

And I say that with experience.

But let me say it again: unlike me, not everyone lapses or relapses.

Many just walk away and never look back.

Notes:

(Use this space to scribble anything that strikes a chord.

An idea, a plan, or even a feeling.

This space is yours)

Show Vulnerability, Seek Help

Have you ever flown a kite?

I have. I am no expert, but I did it as a kid.

In my hometown, during festivals, rooftops turned into kite-flying zones.

Anyone could compete with anyone in the colourful skies.

Just get your kite airborne.

And me?

Struggling. Couldn't even get mine off the ground.

So, I asked someone for help.

That person stood at a distance, holding the kite tied to the string I held tightly.

He waited for my signal, then hurled it into the sky.

And it flew.

In our local lingo, this was called **Churaiya.**

And the hardest part suddenly felt easy.

Once it was in the air, all I had to do was control it with my fingers.

Loosen the string. Pull back.

Let it dance.

That's what asking for help feels like.

Someone standing with you at the most challenging point.

Not holding your hand forever—

Just helping you lift off.

But we don't ask, do we?

We try to play solo.

This makes quitting harder than it needs to be.

We confuse help with weakness.

It's not.

It's strength.

It's awareness.

It's how you win.

And sometimes, it's how you win **easily**.

I've written about this in my book *Vulnerability Intelligence (Vi)*—

That showing vulnerability isn't weakness.

It's strength.

And often, it takes real courage.

But still, most people don't share the vulnerability.

They don't open up.

They're afraid it'll make them look weak.

People often think -

"Why should I tell anyone about what I'm going through?"

Well, talk about it.

You don't need to tell everyone.

Just the ones who genuinely care.

Your well-wishers.

Or even the ones who've been asking you to quit in the first place.

Start there.

When I quit smoking, I told my wife candidly.

"This might be tough for me. I may get mood swings and If I do—please ignore it. Just need that support from you"

When quitting alcohol, I asked for a favour.

"Could you avoid cooking foods that trigger cravings for the first few days?" I was referring to spicy food and the little accessories that had become part of my drinking ritual.

A few more things, and that was it.

Simple conversation.

But it helped a lot. When someone knows what you're going through, they can actually support you with empathy.

Emotionally. Practically. Even Silently.

You're not alone in the fight anymore.

I told my smoker friends,

"I can't smoke anymore. My BP shot up. Something's going on with my lungs."

Was it true? Not really.

I lied. I manipulated.

But I knew this would only work with my duffer friends I loved.

In a way, I *was* asking for their help.

By asking them *not* to screw up my effort.

And you know what?

Most people step back when you bring up medical stuff.

It shuts them up.

But there are always a few sons of guns—the ones who will still offer you a puff, a peg, or try to pull you back with a stupid smile.

Those people?

They're not your friends. Not even close.

They will not understand.

They are the ones to be avoided and blocked.

Hated. Kicked, maybe—I am joking, but I felt like it, once.

But it helps when you actually tell people *exactly* what kind of help you need.

No ambiguity. Specific support.

It could be as simple as:

- I might skip get-togethers and parties for a while.

- Can we remove the triggers from the house?

- Don't worry if I seem moody—it's just withdrawals. Nothing personal.

At home, this clarity matters. Because no one's a mind reader.

And here's the big one. The one that makes people feel awkward:

Seeking medical help.

Quitting gutkha or smoking with a doctor's help?

Some people show up from nowhere —

"Really? Do you need a doctor for that? People quit on their own."

And when it's alcohol? Some people might assume that you must have got into extremes.

They won't just *think* it—some will *say* it. To your face. Or behind your back. Or to someone close to you.

If you ever meet such people, here's my suggestion:

Just tell them—Buzz off.

And yes, I'm being sober when I say that.

You don't need that kind of energy.

You're doing something deeply personal. Something that takes guts.

And nothing else matters. Not their opinion.

On a Serious Note—Seeking Medical Help Matters

Let me tell you why.

Your friend, your spouse, your family—they care. But they often don't *really* understand what substances like tobacco and alcohol do to you.

They might know about how harmful they are.

They might say, "It's bad for your health."

But they might not know *how* these things can manipulate our system.

That's why quitting isn't just about willpower. It's about knowing what you're up against and dealing with.

And for that—you need someone who actually *knows about it.*

A qualified doctor. Someone who understands addiction from the inside out.

It could be your local doctor, a psychologist, a psychiatrist. At times, we don't need to wait till it gets 'bad enough.' Maybe.

And if you're not keen to meet someone face-to-face, find authentic Online support for the substances. These days, the government has also made that available.

Let me share my story. I consulted a clinical Psychologist to quit Gutkha. It helped. Though it was just a few sessions lasting over a month. Smoking I quit on my own using my learnings from quitting Gutkha.

Alcohol, again, I consulted Psychiatrist, who specialised in addiction recovery. I lapsed twice during the consultation, but with help, I could get back stronger.

Support works.

Believe me.

Notes:

(Use this space to scribble anything that strikes a chord.
An idea, a plan, or even a feeling.
This space is yours)

Practice Mindfulness

When I quit gutkha, cigarettes, and alcohol—I made one thing very clear to myself.

I would be mindful of my thoughts.

And I would keep it simple.

I would silently tell myself, without waiting for a craving to hit me:

'I accept myself just as I am. I accept the way I am, completely.

I don't judge my past.

With every breath, I am getting free.'

The most interesting part is that mindfulness reduced my cravings by nearly 70% to 80%.

I don't know how it happened.

But I know this—it felt better. It felt easy.

Curious, I looked up if there was any research behind this—and to my surprise, there was plenty.

One study suggested that mindfulness practices, similar to those in Buddhist models of craving, might offer unique results—not just in reducing cravings but also in stopping them.

Another research showed a significant drop in relapse rates for those who practised mindfulness.

And let me say this—being mindful is not complicated.

Freedom is already inside me, and mindfulness just makes me aware of it.

Let me share one more moment which I can still recall.

A Poolside craving.

One evening, not long after I had quit alcohol, I went for a swim.

It was breezy. There was something naturally romantic about the air and the sky—and honestly, inside me, too.

As I stepped into the water, I noticed the dim lights glowing from the pool walls, reflecting through the transparent blue water.

I stood there, holding the railing—cool water upto the waist and the upper half catching that soft chill of approaching winter.

The wind played with my hair.

There was a table and a couple of chairs by the poolside.

And suddenly—there it was.

A thought.

"Alcohol could have made everything feel better, and I am missing it."

That thought could have easily amplified.

But I caught it.

Because I was mindful.

Now let me ask—was the swimming pool the trigger?

Maybe. Maybe not.

The pool wasn't doing anything. Nor was the breeze, the water, or the lights.

The real trigger was inside me—my mind could have sensed my weaker moments connected to something from the past.

That's the secret about triggers.

They are not always about what we see.

They could also be about what our brain remembers feeling or what it convinces us to feel.

And mindfulness doesn't just help you notice it.

It helps you pause.

Take it easy.

And not fall into the trap.

The Brainwave Study

There's an experiment I read about.

A person who had given up addiction was made to experience how craving changes our brain signals. After wearing the wires on the head tied with the monitor machine, they were asked to *crave* their substance—and instantly, the graph spiked.

Then, they were asked to meditate.

And what happened? The brain waves softened.

That's what our thoughts can do. Mindfulness calms the storm before it turns into destruction. Easily.

Now, I don't mean you have to sit cross-legged for 45 minutes when I talk about mindfulness or meditation.

Because freedom is already inside you, mindfulness makes you aware of it.

Choose what works for you.

Even one minute of breathing with some honest self-talk can be powerful.

Say it your way.

Make it feel like yours.

And another important piece—

Write down what you feel is important.

I did this during the first few months.

Sacrosanct.

Transparent. Raw. Heartfelt.

You get to *see* what's really triggering you.

Sometimes, it could be a thought.

Sometimes a memory.

Sometimes, a misbelief you didn't realise.

When you put your emotions or beliefs on paper, it gets easier to question them.

To settle them.

To heal them.

You don't have to write every hour.

But when something muddles with your emotions or efforts, pause and write.

Even a few words.

You'll be surprised how much clarity shows up once the noise is on the page and not just in your head.

Universal truth - Even the doctors who help with addictions ask to do it.

And they are right. I vouch for it.

Because The goal is not to build a wall around cravings. The goal is to see them, acknowledge them and learn to make them irrelevant. They will stop showing up. That's where freedom begins.

That's where healing starts.

That's mindfulness.

Notes:

(Use this space to scribble anything that strikes a chord.
    An idea, a plan, or even a feeling.
    This space is yours)

Mindfulness, in the context of addiction, is an emotional audit, free from judgment.

The Triggers

Internal Triggers

I realised something about triggers that I must share with you. You may even feel like you already know it.

Just like all roads lead home,

'all emotions can lead to a craving.'

Now, where can we divert them?

That's on us.

Let's do a reality check.

A bad day at work.

I had a rough conversation with my boss.

I felt upset.

Then I felt angry.

Then I started feeling awful.

And right after that—I had a trigger.

I needed that Gutkha, smoke or alcohol.

Stuck in traffic.

I was driving back home.

The road was jammed. I felt restless.

Then I got irate at some traffic criminal who just committed a crime by breaking traffic rules.

That turned into anxiety.

And a few moments later … I needed that Gutkha, smoke or alcohol.

An evening Walk.

I was tired after dinner, just taking a stroll.

I remembered something good I'd done that day.

Felt bloated with pride.

Felt peace.

And even then—a trigger.

I needed that Gutkha, smoke or alcohol.

Triggers don't just come from stress.

They can come from almost any emotion—good, bad, or even a confused state of mind.

A person walking beside me wouldn't even know what was happening inside.

But I would.

And that's the whole point.

If the trigger begins inside me.

Then I have the power to redirect them.

Emotional awareness is my steering wheel.

Let me share it with a visual, as I believe visuals add some value, too.

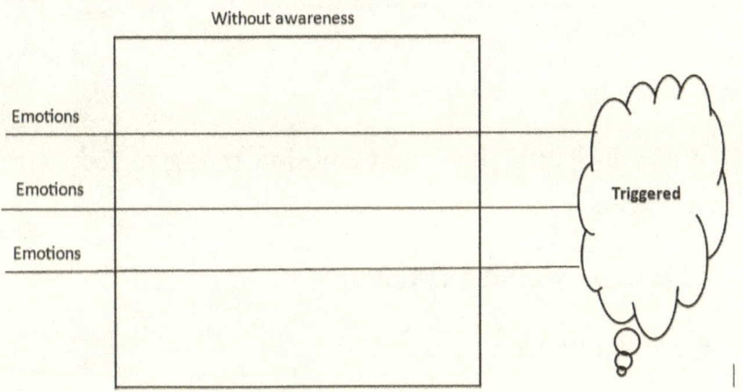

When emotions go unchecked, they trigger cravings for the substance.

But as we build emotional self-awareness, we begin to see the triggers—and they slowly lose their power. But they can do it again at any time in the future, which makes it important to stay mindful—just it.

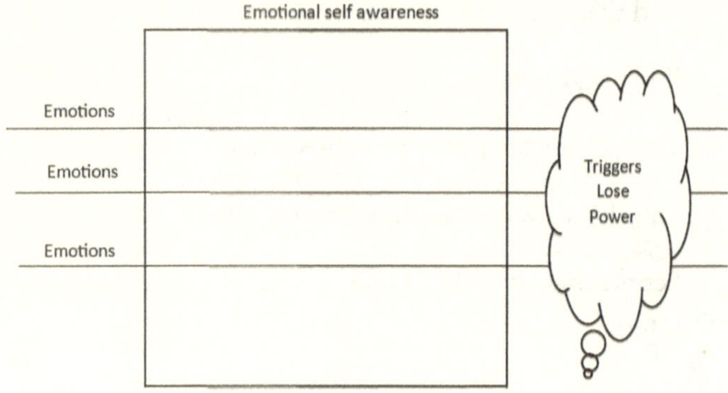

Now, you might wonder—

What do I do if I see that emotion trying to seduce me with a craving.

That's a very valid question.

Because I've been there.

And here's what helped me:

- I reached out to my *WHYs*—those strong, personal reasons I had written down. The ones that felt like war cries—loud, burning, and mine.

- I didn't just read them. I felt them again.

- I revisited some of my worst memories—the ones that had made me want to quit. There were many.

The point is: KILL THE TRIGGERS.

Right there.

Right then.

If a craving is about emotions, fight it with an even stronger emotions—

anger, guilt, grief, disgust—whatever works.

But never take a craving for granted.

They don't go easy. They might come back with vengeance for some time.

- I also learned to hold space for myself.

- To sit still and let the trigger burn out on its own.

- Because we are born to be stronger than our cravings.

Yes, I have much more to share on handling triggers— including one surprisingly powerful strategy.

But let's go slow.

Deep but slow.

No rush—unless you really have to.

Let me tell you about two cats my friend had. He told me that he suddenly became fond of cats and showed a lot of excitement while sharing about them. He described them so beautifully as if the two cats were in front of me. He told me that both lived in the same cat house at his home, and he loved them very much.

The black one was dominating and aggressive, always ready for a fight, making that look scary.

The white one was different. It was a bit reserved but very strong. It mostly kept to itself, playing quietly with the toys in the corner.

Curious, I asked him,

"But what happens if they fight each other? Which one wins?"

He looked at me, smiled, and said something very interesting.

"The one I feed more... wins."

It made so much sense.

The more I feed the craving, the more powerful it gets.

The more I feed my WHYs, the stronger they become.

It was as simple as that, isn't it?

If I ask you—why did you quit tobacco or alcohol?

Would you say because you *got infatuated with it?*

No. Never.

You quit because you *hated* it.

And deep down, you knew—it wasn't joy. It was an ambush.

And you also know this—

Even the ones who are still addicted to them … they want to quit.

They don't enjoy it either.

They possibly have not yet figured out that they can have more fun and joy without them.

I quit because I never liked them.

The smelly hands from smoking.

The stained teeth from Gutkha.

The self-injected highs of alcohol kept me away from real joys and made my productive hours of the day shorter.

Internal triggers might get spiked by something external, but they often create themselves.

They show up out of habit, out of pattern, out of nowhere.

And it may not end here.

The triggers come from what we *see, smell,* or *hear*—the external ones.

Notes:

(Use this space to scribble anything that strikes a chord.
An idea, a plan, or even a feeling.
This space is yours)

External Triggers

If you ask, was there a trigger when I first saw someone drinking or smoking?

Absolutely not. Because I was not yet addicted and there was no connection.

But yes, I was just curious why others did it.

That's it.

Let me ask you something again.

How was the *first* taste of alcohol? or

How was that *first* drag of a cigarette?

Let me answer for myself.

The first taste of alcohol was awful. Because it was never good, for most of us.

I used to think—how can anyone even like it?

It was the same with gutkha. Same with cigarettes.

And yet—I fell for them.

And later, I *craved* them.

I got triggered just by seeing someone else smoking or drinking.

Now, talking about **external triggers**—

They're real. And they'll be around.

Our brain starts connecting memories and feelings and even relating emotions to the things we *see* again and again.

Let me give an old-school example. I once searched for the best cars available below 10 lacs as I was planning to buy one. My old car had started asking for a lot of repairs.

And you know what? My Facebook, Google, and every other platform started showing a lot of car advertisements and articles.

Both of us can tell that this was nothing but a digital market stunt.

But honestly, getting triggered for alcohol or smoking is not different if we feed our mind when we see someone enjoying as they smoke or drink.

And that's the irony.

All external triggers could be both living and non-living.

Like someone having them.

Someone who adds to the old memories with it

Someone whose presence could take us into that zone.

Movies where actors glorify them

Shops that sell them and so on.

Even the ashtrays, the perfume used after smoking in the car or those food items that come along with alcohol

And your triggers may be completely different from mine.

They're personal.

Emotional.

Unpredictable.

Now, you may ask—while we've talked about handling internal triggers, what do we do about external ones since we don't have much control over them?

Let me say this—**every external trigger eventually becomes an internal one.**

If someone smoking doesn't move something inside you, it's no longer a trigger.

So, the question becomes—**how do we make external triggers irrelevant… before they become internal ones?**

Here's what helped me.

To start with, **avoid being near those triggers as much as possible.**

Shops that sell them.

Keeping them at home.

I threw away every last bit of those things every time before I quit.

I remember the moment—I poured the bottles into the bathroom wash basin.

For many, it can be a painful sight.

Let me confess—it pained me, too.

Why?

I don't know.

But today, I would call it the **right thing to do**.

I even avoided standing around people who were having gutkha, cigarettes, or alcohol.

Not because I was scared.

But because I realised that **I was being strong.**

Because *sometimes strength is all about walking away before it gets late.*

I would even avoid conversations about it.

Again—not out of fear.

It was just about staying focused.

It's like this—

When you plant a small sapling, you build a small fence around it.

You give it water. You protect it from winds and storms.

You let it grow roots.

And one day… it becomes a tree.

It stands strong on its own.

Then, you sit in its shade and enjoy its fruits and the fruit of your hard work, as it no longer needs that protection.

I invite you to pause for a moment and visualise how a sapling becomes a giant tree.

Or simply look at the photo.

Isn't it magical how nature grows—quietly, patiently, and so beautifully?

It's eco-friendly—good for the environment, and for us too.

Water

Protect

Feed

Care

This journey is the same.

It's about patience.

Discipline.

Commitment to something you've started

And, when I was ready, I started ignoring triggers with a neutral frame of mind.

When you have gutkha shops right outside your home, accepting their presence itself felt empowering.

The people selling them weren't trying to add more addicts to the world—they were simply making a living. Right or wrong? I don't know.

With time, even walking past those shops to buy something else didn't bother me.

I felt that smokers and those buying alcohol at shops would probably learn about the harm they are inflicting on themselves one day.

That's it, what I felt.

And after some time, even that empathy for them stopped. Not because I changed but because I realised my empathy doesn't help them.

The external trigger slowly faded out.

But, I never dropped the guards.

Notes:

(Use this space to scribble anything that strikes a chord.
An idea, a plan, or even a feeling.
This space is yours)

Just One Last Time (The Myth)

Professional negotiators often use this subtle technique to keep the conversation going—just long enough to get what they want.

It's quiet. Strategic. Powerful.

Kind of like the shopkeeper who shouts out as you are walking away:

"Madam, Just try this once—you'll love it. It's in high demand."

Or the customer service executive who jumps in just before you escalate a complaint -

"Sir, give us one last chance. We won't disappoint you—I promise, I will handle it personally."

It works.

More often than we realize.

And addiction? It does the same.

Because they're not just talking.

They're negotiating.

And guess what?

When your craving makes you believe,

"Just one last time… and then I will quit,"

it's doing the exact same thing.

It's a pitch.

A trap disguised.

"One last time" is never just one.

So, if it shows up with that offer,

Avoid negotiation or arguments.

Just walk away.

Because the moment you engage,

you're not winning—

Why?

Because your conscious mind is trying to win a negotiation with a powerful subconscious mind. And we all know who wins in such a combat.

You may not be surprised—but let me tell you, it's happened to me more times than I can count.

That "one last time"?

It was always me negotiating with myself.

And I only lost.

Every. Single. Time.

That's the trap.

Trap, Trap and Trap.

Once you see that clearly,

you stop falling for it.

And it can come in many forms. Let me share a few.

A few months after I quit, I was at a party.

A friend—still drinking—came up to me. He was a bit tipsy.

He didn't ask me to have one drink.

But he said something that sounded like a trap -

"Bro, even doctors say one drink a day is fine. Even traffic rules allow little while driving."

To me, he sounded silly, cheesy and a manipulator. Traffic rules do not allow anything.

But let's be honest—that one line could've been enough to pull me back in.

The best reply I gave him?

"Maybe for them who need it."

Simple. Neutral.

Fuck off.

What I was really doing was this—

I didn't agree or disagree.

Because if I agreed, even slightly,

my subconscious would log it—

and bring it up at a weaker moment.

That's how these thoughts sneak in.

One casual comment can ruin all hard work.

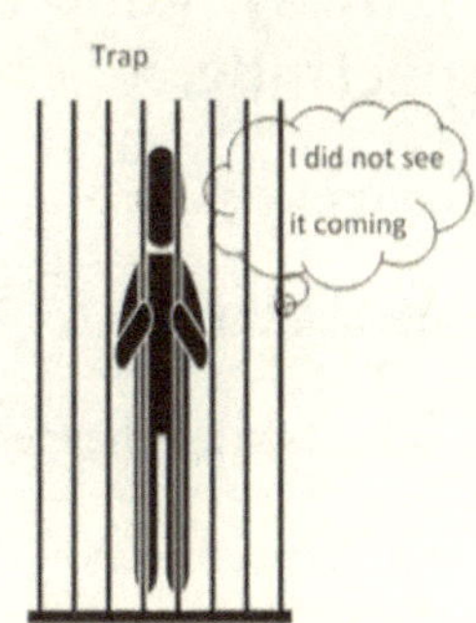

And then some people say things like:

"You're no fun since you stopped drinking."

Let me be blunt.

They are your worst well-wishers.

Not because they're bad people.

But because they don't understand what we are going through.

Sometimes, it can be even someone in a position of power—like your boss.

They might hand you a drink and say, looking at your eyes,

"Come on, just one sip."

I've seen that, too, in real life.

The best thing to do?

Step away. Keep that glass, or give it back respectfully.

You don't owe anyone an explanation.

Just be firm.

Chances are—they're just trying to make a connection.

But that connection does nothing for you.

So, at the cost of being repetitive, let me say again.

"Just once."

"One last time."

"One won't make you addicted."

"One can't give you cancer or a heart attack."

On and on and on...

It's a trap.

I knew if I started once, it wouldn't stop.

The best way I found to handle it was being prepared for it.

So when someone actually said it—

Be immune.

And I made sure—**I never argued.**

Because arguing gives the thought a life.

Silence starves it.

Let me share how I once fell for the trap—despite everything I knew.

I was under a lot of pressure.

Work stress. Deadlines. Commitments at work.

And in the middle of all that, something told me—it was my inner voice.

"A drink might help. Just a little one. You've earned it."

But, I had already quit.

I had made it through the hardest part.

But on the 11th day, I gave in.

So, I poured myself 30 ml. Thought it would be the last without any guilt.

But within minutes, I thought:

'What's the point of 30?'

I poured another 60.

And before I knew it, I had finished 300 ml.

All in one night.

Next day?

I felt **Guilty. Ashamed. Angry. Tired.**

Tired of myself.

What hurt most was the knowing—

I had done the hard part. I had held on for 10 days.

And I threw it all away because I believed **"just one"** would be harmless.

I didn't quit again.

I told myself I would quit next week, but I didn't.

Until one day when I made it.

So remember—there is nothing like one last time, remember it is an UNDO button we have in digital sheets. It will undo whatever you have done.

Don't press it. Because you have pressed the reset button and you don't want to undo it.

Notes:

*(Use this space to scribble anything that strikes a chord.
An idea, a plan, or even a feeling.
This space is yours)*

Reinventing Yourself

Handling the Boredom After Quitting

Boredom—or what feels like a void—is one of the most common things people go through about after quitting. So, it is often a normal experience.

But here's what no one usually tells you.

That boredom you're feeling?

It's not because alcohol or tobacco are gone.

That boredom was always there.

Maybe you just didn't feel it.

Addictions are good at helping you escape the reality. They numb, distract, and fog that emptiness.

So, that feeling may not have been caused after quitting.

It just got into awareness.

And now, you get a chance to fix it.

Yes, I'm calling it boredom or a void—because that's what I called it, too.

But what is it truly?

It's an opportunity.

An opportunity to fill that void with something that brings real peace.

Not by some chemicals which hit the mind.

But peace. Real emotions.

A better sense of things is needed to make better decisions.

And, let me not get into brain chemicals and neurotransmitters, as I know nothing about them.

Zilch.

Yes, they got triggered by alcohol and tobacco.

But our body knows how to recuperate, and the mind knows how to heal.

Just like your pupils adjust to the light, or your skin adjusts to summer and winter—

Your brain adjusts, too.

It just needs time and some attention.

So what now?

What do you do with that emptiness.?

You address it meaningfully.

Like that tightrope walker.

One step. One thought. One day at a time.

Don't look down. Don't look back.

Now, some people say they didn't feel any void.

That they quit, still hung out with friends who smoked or drank—and enjoyed.

Let me tell you—maybe they're telling the truth.

Maybe that worked for them.

But we're all different, and I don't feel ashamed of telling you that I didn't dare to go back to the same friends who partied in the evenings with air filled with smoke and smelled of alcohol.

Never till I was ready.

Also, there's no trophy for going back and sitting with the old gang.

There's no medal for testing your limits.

I chose a safe and stronger path.

We have not been doing this for a moment. We're doing it for life.

That said, let me share everything I did during this time— not as advice or a prescription.

Because you and I—we've had different experiences, different perspectives, and different challenges.

But we do have one thing in common.

And that one thing matters more than anything else.

We both hate alcohol, smoking, or gutkha.

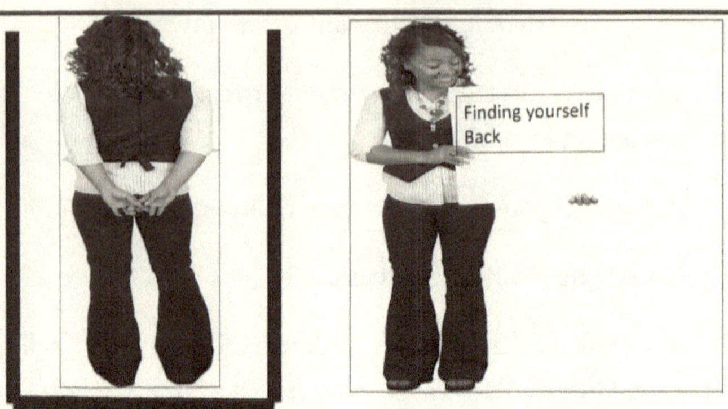

Addiction to escape from Boredom   Breaking free from Addictions

The visual above shares how addiction keeps us from reality and boredom by giving us artificial highs. For the same reason, once we quit them, we feel lonely or feel that we are missing something meaningful.

So, I did the following to stay focused on why I started:

- I became more spiritually inclined.

- I meditated regularly.

- I did physical activities like walking, swimming, trekking, and even short marathons.

- I started writing books.

- I spent more time with my family.

- I listened to music that lifted me up.

- I watched TV

- I practised gratitude.

- I took one day at a time—not life.

I will expand on these because each one helped me in a different way. Also, I suggest 'do what works for you', and you are most welcome to follow what worked for me.

I Became More Spiritually Inclined

Being spiritual means different things to different people.

It often means being religious, staying sin-free, speaking softly, and being poised in the community around me.

But I don't know how to keep sin-free.

Sometimes, I lie—to my wife for peace.

To my boss, for avoiding a faceoff.

And to myself… for that sinful ice cream after dinner.

For me, spirituality meant something different.

Clarity about my life is heading to. Stillness that helps me see better.

A saint once asked,

"If I give you a bamboo ladder to climb a wall, how would you use your IQ?"

One disciple said, "I would use it to find the correct angle so the ladder stays stable."

The saint nodded. "Correct. And how would you use your EQ?"

Another replied, "To manage my fear while climbing."

"Right again," the saint said. "Now—how would you use your spiritual quotient?"

The disciples fell silent.

Then the saint said,

"Spiritual quotient is knowing whether your ladder is on the right wall. What if you climb all the way up, only to realise it was the wrong wall? That's what spirituality is—knowing what matters and aligning your life."

That story hit me hard.

Because when I looked inside, I realised something clearly.

I didn't want to be remembered as an alcoholic or chain smoker.

I didn't want to die of cancer or a heart attack brought on by the substances.

I wanted to live a healthy and independent life until my last day.

To walk on my own, use the restroom on my own, and die with dignity.

When I started aligning with that intention, the noise addictions went silent.

In that stillness, I began to see better, what is right and what is not.

I Meditated (Sort Of, But It Worked)

Let me confess—I never meditated for more than five minutes a day.

But I followed a simple format that made all the difference.

I would close my eyes and start by focusing on my breath.

Then, I would slowly count to ten.

And after that, I would go somewhere in my mind—a place that brought me peace.

For me, it was a small restaurant in the hills.

I imagined myself sitting there in the early evening, well dressed in a suit, sipping black coffee, eating an omelette, soft pipe music playing in the background, and watching the quiet valley below.

That image calmed everything.

When I opened my eyes, everything felt still. Settled.

I don't even know how it relates to addressing boredom, but it helped me find a quiet place inside.

And sometimes, that's all we need.

You don't need to be an expert at meditation.

You just need to find *your* peaceful space—even if it exists only in your imagination.

I would call it meditation any day.

I did physical activities like walking, swimming, trekking, and even short marathons.

Experts say that exercise releases the same chemicals that alcohol or tobacco triggered to make us feel better.

Honestly, I didn't care about that.

I knew one thing—every time I exercised, I felt better, healthier, and like I was doing something that would keep me standing strong until old age—on my own legs, strong bones, joints, and muscles.

Swimming in water felt like hitting reset, which I was trying to do by quitting. Trekking brought me closer to nature—I could feel the wind, the silence, and 100% real nature. These days, I see so many people my age, 55, walking up the hills. And every single time, it gives me joy after completing one trek.

Even walking a narrow two-foot-wide trail, by the side of a hill, carved naturally by trekkers, felt like an adventure. At that moment, it was no less than Everest. My adrenaline gave me a high that no alcohol or gutkha could ever give.

Same with the 10K marathons.

The best part?

Clicking a selfie with a finisher medal around the neck and posting it on some Whatsapp groups to show off felt so satisfying.

I started writing books.

To confess, it wasn't something that happened right after I quit gutkha, smoking, or alcohol. It's something I've been doing over the last few years.

But I want to share this because it helped.

It gave me a space to express and organise my thoughts. It actually made my inner dialogues clearer—like I could feel and see them every time I fell into a pattern of wrong self-talk.

And honestly, we all don't have to write books.

Just writing down your thoughts—stories, poems, even a quick journaling while playing with words... is more than enough to go beyond that void you feel after quitting.

I spent more time with my family.

I read this somewhere: When people in old age were asked, *"What do you regret the most?"*

Most of them said, *"I wish I could've spent more time with my family."*

And honestly, we all know this truth before we grow old.

We just forget it somewhere along the way.

Spending time with your parents, your sons or daughters, and watching them grow could be one of the most meaningful things you ever do.

But somewhere, addictions came in the way.

Of all the things I did during this phase, I feel spending time with my family was the most unwinding and self-rewarding.

Playing quiz with my daughters, spending a full day just being together—it's priceless.

You know that, too.

I listened to music that lifted me up.

Thanks to those great inventions, we don't need a cassette or a giant music system to listen to music anymore.

If someone peeked into my music app, they'd find at least a thousand songs—everything from the '70s, '80s, and even the latest ones.

Some songs remind me of good times in school.

Some take me back to the days when I mimicked movie stars.

Music is a boon.

A true gift from God to mankind.

I played karaoke. I lip-synced. I made videos and posted them on Facebook.

I listened while walking, trekking, and even when I was falling asleep.

And honestly—how can anyone feel a void when there's music?

It's a treasure of creativity. It soothes the mind. It calms the soul.

I don't think anyone would disagree with me on that.

I Watched TV

Binge-watching didn't seem bad anymore—

because I didn't sleep drunk somewhere between the movies,

and I watched the same movie later without recalling the story.

Romantic and suspense genres felt so much more engaging.

I even started going to theatres again—

popcorn tub, salted and caramel mixed, a chilled Coke by the side.

Waiting for a new release like I used to in my school days.

Honestly, it felt like life was rewinding.

Whatever that means—but it did feel so.

I Practiced Gratitude

Gratitude helped me fill that void.

It acts like a silent antidote to the emotional pain that often comes with that boredom or emptiness.

And here's the truth—gratitude isn't some one-time moment of saying "thank you."

It's a way of being. A practice. A mindset.

Many people make it a habit to find just one or two things every day to be thankful for—some even write them down.

That's not just some emotional thing. It becomes part of your values. A mental muscle.

Research and studies also show that people who regularly feel and show gratitude tend to be happier, more successful, and emotionally stable.

Gratitude doesn't need to be about big things.

It could be for simple things—like a warm meal, a phone call, a moment of peace, or a walk.

It could also be about the courage you've shown by quitting…

and the people standing by you.

You don't need a reason to be grateful.

You just need a moment to notice what's still *good*.

I Took One Day at a Time—Not Life

The boredom hits harder when you start thinking that your whole life is going to be like this.

That same dull feeling. Forever.

It's the kind of thinking that multiplies the emptiness. I've been there.

Remember the COVID lockdowns?

Months at home. Nothing to do. Life felt stuck and clueless.

But we got through it.

How?

We had hope.

Sure, the hope came from fear—fear of the unknown, fear of what could happen.

But it still helped us live *one day at a time.*

And it's the same thing after quitting addictions.

There's fear—of going back, giving in again, and relapsing.

But if we stay with just today, we keep that hope alive.

I didn't overthink the future.

I didn't sit wondering", How will I enjoy festivals, weddings, and weekends without a drink or smoke?"

Those questions slowly stopped appearing.

Why?

Because each day became its own reward.

The pride of staying away.

Even just for a day.

Was what I needed.

As promised, I've shared every bit of how I quit my addictions.

And I have more to share.

Notes:

(Use this space to scribble anything that strikes a chord.
An idea, a plan, or even a feeling.
This space is yours)

Cutting the Emotional Chord

I was watching a film shoot.

The director kept yelling, "Cut!" after every take.

What exactly was he cutting? Nothing.

He could have just said "OK" or "done." But why "cut"?

The way I saw it, he likely meant: 'Stop the act. It's done.'

And that's how I see cutting emotional chords.

Just say Cut.

To say, 'I'm done.'

To say, 'Stop your performance. I'm not recording anymore. Your scene's over. You're done here.'

Going further, cutting that connection with addictions could be just like losing past memories with them.

While losing past memories is figurative—we can't actually do that (or everyone would've done it by now).

Just click a button and

Ta-da

Cravings gone, mama.

But there have been some real observations—

In cases of severe memory loss, like advanced dementia, cravings are not the same.

They change.

So, the point here is -

Addictions are deeply connected to our memories and emotions.

We don't have to lose our memory to get free. Not possible.

But we can just choose to break the link between emotions and addiction.

That's certainly possible.

On a serious note, let me share what it took to cut that emotional chord.

It started with one thing:

Facing the truth.

Bringing my real past with addictions into awareness.

Not ignoring the past emotions.

I asked myself honestly:

How many times have I connected addiction with support, joy, celebration, liberation, unwinding, and more?

Just for discussion, let's say I did that a thousand times.

Those moments were wired into my head.

So now, to cut the chord with a thousand emotional links, I needed something even more powerful.

And I found it.

I feel that love, as an emotion, is so connecting and huge.

But when used right, some emotions are even more powerful.

- Hatred

- Anger

- Disgust

When I used these emotions to break the old emotional links with addiction, it helped.

Maybe unknowingly, I was using neuroscience.

The brain's reward system remembers what brought pleasure.

But when you hit it back—with disgust, with anger—

it's no longer a pleasure.

It becomes pain.

Like someone who has made a lot of money in the stock market, he would find it a good option to invest and achieve whatever in life, but one day, the market crashes and continues to decline for a month.

He lost more money than he made, and he started hating the stock market with disgust. Even the mention of it creates disgust. It is no longer a pleasure; it is like an acute pain for him.

Same way, alcohol, smoking, and gutkha addictions—all began to feel like a curse to me.

So go ahead.

Feel the anger.

Cut the chord.

End the scene.

You're the director now.

But let me say this, too:

Sometimes, people believe they've broken all emotional connections with addiction—

yet they relapse.

Why?

Because this isn't a one-time "Cut!" like in a film shoot.

This isn't a single scene.

It's a series of scenes.

It needs multiple takes to make your movie—

Your story,

Your narrative,

Your freedom.

It needs—Mindfulness, Repetition, Awareness

It might take weeks. Or months.

But it can be done.

Here's what helped me—and it's practical:

Start writing.

Whenever a craving hits, pause and note:

- What just happened?

- What were you feeling?

- What triggered the thought of alcohol, gutkha, or smoke?

Say you just got a promotion, and suddenly—

"Let's celebrate with a drink."

Write it down.

Do this for a week.

Now take that list you just made.

And refer back to your WHY list—The hero of the movie, everything roots back to him.

The list filled with the raw truth, the disgust, the anger.

The one you wrote when you said enough is enough.

Hold those reasons in front of every link on your craving list.

And one by one—break the link.

This is not about telling yourself that the link never existed.

This is about emotionally losing the connection.

Even the bad guys die in the movies.

Addictions

Break the

Emotional Chord

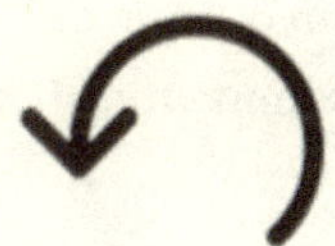

Undo Addictions

Notes:

(Use this space to scribble anything that strikes a chord.
An idea, a plan, or even a feeling.
This space is yours)

Breaking the Subconscious Connection

I have shared most of what can help in quitting—from my experience and from falling in and out of addictions many times.

But what's so different about what I'm about to say now?

This helped me big time.

This is what held me back from going back.

This is what helped me stay quit.

Easily. Effortlessly.

Because here's the hard truth, as I mentioned earlier—willpower doesn't work.

We are somehow made to believe it does.

But when we side with willpower in a battle against addiction,

we're most certainly setting ourselves up to lose.

Willpower sits in the conscious mind.

Addiction lives in the colossally big subconscious.

And that thing?

It doesn't care about the rationale.

It doesn't care about your commitments.

It runs on habit, memory, emotion—or all of it.

It runs on what we've fed it over time.

And in this battle?

The subconscious will win.

Every damn time.

Until… you break that subconscious connection.

And here's the million-dollar question:

How the hell do we break that subconscious connection?

Believe me—it's not as hard as we make it out to be.

It's just that we fed that horrible stuff to our subconscious for years.

If we start feeding it something new, it will again believe it.

Let's start with something simple.

Start With This Exercise

Think about a cocktail party or a celebration where alcohol was being served—one where you had a gala time.

Not too long ago.

Let that memory come back—just for a minute.

Don't overthink it. Replay it like a movie in your mind.

What did you see and feel?

Did you feel the warmth around you?

The fun, the joy, the laughter, the cheerful voices?

Did you smell the alcohol, the tobacco smoke?

Felt those vibes?

Those memories are part of the subconscious and is registered with the visuals, voices, smells, and emotions connected with those addictions.

And that's how all of them guktha, cigarettes, alcohol—are in the subconscious.

And somewhere down the line, we started linking these things with everything we wanted to feel.

Joy.

Confidence.

Relaxation.

Building relationships and even socialising.

But that's an illusion.

With that illusion, even the smell of alcohol or tobacco or the sight of people enjoying it can pull us right back in.

Not because we're weak.

But because of that subconscious connection.

Let Me Share Three Methods That Actually Worked for Me

1. Rotten Egg

   Some may find this rudimentary—maybe even disgusting.

   And that the whole idea.

   But believe me, it worked like emotional surgery for me.

   A complete surgical procedure.

   And I did this—

   I broke open two eggs and poured them into a bottle.

   Capped it.

   Left it or rather hid it somewhere in the house for two to three days.

   The eggs started to rot.

   They change colour.

   They changed texture.

   And the smell?

   Absolutely, absolutely repulsive. Enough to make anyone to puke.

   Now comes the important part.

I brought the substance I was addicted to—gutkha, a cigarette, or alcohol—right in front of me.

Held it in one hand. Smelled it. Craved it.

And with the other, I opened that bottle of rotting egg.

And smelled the stench.

It made me gag.

It made me feel like puking.

And that's okay.

That's the point.

I repeated this.

And, every time the craving hit—I would Open the bottle.

Smell the rotten eggs.

Hold the disgust. Let that disgust sink in

Repeat ten times or may be more

Do it once every day for a week.

What happened by the end of the week?

Just the thought or smell of those substances led to disgust. Only disgust.

You can do this again anytime after a week as well.

Rot a new egg.

Rot the old habit with it.

And break that damn connection.

2. Visual Disconnection

Here's another one that worked.

Think of something you just can't stand to look at.

You don't need to tell anyone what it is.

Just thinking about it makes you feel like puking.

Maybe it's something gross. Maybe it's something stinking or reeking.

Whatever it is, let it be real to you.

Now, take a printout of that image.

Yes, an actual picture. Have it with you.

Do the same exercise as before.

Get the substance—gutkha, a cigarette, or alcohol—right in front of you.

Hold it in one hand.

And on the other, keep that picture ready.

Look at the substance.

Then, look at the image.

Repeat.

Again and again.

Go slow. Let your senses sink in with the new connection.

Let that picture destroy the craving.

Do it ten times.

Do it every day for a week.

By the end of the week, your brain starts to stitch them together.

The substance and that horrible image.

They start to feel nasty. *Exactly* the reaction we want.

That's your subconscious reprogramming itself.

For me?

The image I chose was so disturbing I started to feel sick even looking at a cigarette.

What was the image?

A photo of human shit rotting in a dark, stinking black sewer.

Disgusting, I know.

But that's the point.

I wanted to see my addiction for what it actually was—behind all the disguise and delusion.

Ugly.

Dirty.

Rotten.

My subconscious couldn't separate the two anymore.

Addiction and filth.

They became one and the same.

3. Snap the Craving

This one's simple.

But *shockingly* effective.

I put a rubber band around my wrist.

Every time a craving tried to pull me back, I pulled the rubber band and snapped it.

Just enough to feel that sting.

Was I punishing myself?

No.

I wasn't trying to hurt myself.

I was interrupting the pattern.

Breaking the subconscious loop from autopilot mode.

I did not set it on autopilot - it was programmed.

I interrupted the code.

The craving learned it the hard way.

And I walked out—the easy way.

Notes:

(Use this space to scribble anything that strikes a chord.
An idea, a plan, or even a feeling.
This space is yours)

Trust Yourself

Let me ask you something.

Peter wants to quit his addiction.

Zara, his friend, knows how to quit, as she was once into smoking and alcohol.

Now, Peter has these four options while he quits.

1. Peter trusts himself, but not Zara.

2. Peter trusts himself and Zara as well.

3. Peter doesn't trust himself but trusts Zara.

4. Peter neither trusts himself nor Zara.

Which of the above options gives Peter the best shot at quitting?

Most would say that if he trusts Zara, she can help him.

But here's the truth—

If Peter doesn't trust himself, nothing else would really matter, not even Zara.

Nothing matters more than trusting oneself.

Let me share another relatable example.

Imagine the beginning of any organisation that has created excellence, such as Amazon, Apple, Starbucks, and Netflix.

We know they all faced ups and downs, setbacks and challenges.

Now let me ask—what was their state of mind when they started?

Probably a dream with conviction, intention, passion, and some trust.

During the most difficult times, when nothing seemed to work, it wasn't only passion or strategy that kept them alive.

It was trust.

Trust in their values.

Trust in what they were building.

Trust in the direction they had chosen.

That's what kept them from giving up.

When quitting addiction, we have a similar journey.

We start with intention and conviction. A firm resolve to quit addictions.

But we still face challenges.

We face withdrawal symptoms, cravings, and doubt.

And in those weak moments, what do we need most?

We need trust.

Trust that what we started is the right thing.

Trust that even if you feel that craving, it will not last. But your intention would.

Trust that withdrawal symptoms don't last forever.

That healing will happen.

And most of all—

Trust that we can do this.

Let me say something debatable and misunderstood by many.

We need to trust that even 30 ml a day is harmful.

That it doesn't add any damn value to our life.

We need to trust that even one drag of a cigarette can cause cancer.

It's not about doing it occasionally or socially.

It's not about how little—it's still poison.

And we need to trust this, too—

That just because everyone is doing it doesn't make it right.

It doesn't make it normal.

And we are not here to be part of the crowd.

And we need to trust that we are responsible for breaking free.

Not society.

Not the system.

Not the doctor.

I am.

We are responsible.

Ask yourself often: What's one moment today when I trusted myself, even a little?

Write it down.

That's your proof.

The mind starts building evidence of trust.

We need to trust ourselves right now.

Even if we have failed before.

Let me ask you—

How often have you met a dead end following a road map app?

Stuck in a narrow lane?

And then you felt upset about why you trusted the app more than your instinct on that particular turn of the road.

Even though something inside you knew that turn didn't feel right.

That's what addiction does, too.

It is like a flawed map we have followed for years.

Which had been telling us—

"This is the way forward."

And we trust it, because we believe that we are in control.

And now we know the truth.

And, deep down, our gut knows the truth.

We just forgot how to trust it.

This makes it important.

The TRUST.

Notes:

*(Use this space to scribble anything that strikes a chord.
An idea, a plan, or even a feeling.
This space is yours)*

Celebrate Small Wins

Please try doing this for one day. Note how many times you thanked people—maybe for opening the door, helping you with something, or giving you a hand—whatever it might be.

I probably thank people a few times a day for their small gestures.

And then, I also asked myself this:

How many times do I thank myself?

Zilch.

Never.

And that's not done.

No SIR.

Why shouldn't I appreciate myself—not just with some casual inner dialogue, but with something more than that?

Let me put it another way:

If we want to promote any behaviour, the best way is to reward it.

Like when a child helps their parents with chores—an affectionate appreciation, a smile, a thank you—it inspires them to help again.

Because a child feels good being seen.

To be valued.

The act of quitting an addiction needs the same.

It might sound naïve to some, especially perfectionists, who only allow themselves to feel accomplished for a reward after completing the whole task.

They're often the hardest on themselves.

But self-appreciation is one powerful way to stay motivated, especially when no one else appreciates you the way you wish to be appreciated.

You are the only one who has been with you in every single step. Celebrate that. Honour that.

How Life Changes When We Quit Addiction

Let me share a real example.

A friend invited me and my family for dinner. He and his wife prepared excellent Punjabi food.

I had quit addictions. I was out of it.

My friend, though, was still into drinking.

Even before dinner began, he'd already had a few drinks. I picked up my juice glass and watched him make himself another drink.

I asked,

"Why are you drinking so much?"

He replied,

"You don't want to drink—good for you. But let me celebrate."

Actually, he had received an increment that day.

That hit me.

Because I remembered how I used to do the same thing.

How celebration used to mean making another drink.

How it didn't feel like a celebration without it.

What changed?

Today, I celebrate with real things.

Things that matter to me: real emotions.

Earned, not influenced.

Sometimes, the best reward is something you have always liked.

For me, it's the simple things:

Going on a hike again without feeling breathless.

Painting.

Swimming.

Buying a nice shirt.

Spending time with my family—dinner, a movie—while present to feel my emotions.

Even if you're still halfway through.

Even if you're still finding it hard at times.

Celebrate anyway.

You have fought battles no one saw. Don't you deserve to thank yourself?

Also, here's What I Realised

Even when I celebrate, I don't get casual.

I don't forget how hard it is.

I remind myself that I am still committed.

And these small wins?

They grow. They build. They make something big.

Like drops of rain that fill a pond.

Notes:

(Use this space to scribble anything that strikes a chord.
    An idea, a plan, or even a feeling.
    This space is yours)

Be Prepared - The World Doesn't Care About Your Quitting

Sounds rude.

I know.

But let's just call it what it is. A spade, a spade.

That's the hard truth most people face when they quit an addiction.

So here's the mindset I wish someone had told me earlier:

Don't wait for anyone to cheer you up.

Don't expect anyone to understand what you're going through.

Expect it to be lonely.

At first, people might say things like, "How brave you are."

Maybe a "Good job" or "Proud of you."

But that's just for a few days.

And you're left facing the same battle: the cravings, the emotional ups and downs.

Life goes back to normal for others.

Not for you, till you completely break free.

You're still waking up every day, trying not to slip back.

Still dealing with cravings that come out of nowhere.

And slowly, you begin to realise—you're mostly on your own in this.

Even the people who love you most might not get it.

Let me tell you something that actually happened.

Once, I was really struggling with cravings. It had been a tough week. I was tired and emotionally drained.

So I told my wife, "I'm finding it really difficult. I don't know how much longer I can hold out without drinking."

She looked at me with love and concern and said,

"Maybe just take a little… so you feel okay?"

And I lapsed back into alcohol.

It wasn't her fault. It was mine.

She just didn't know what addiction felt like.

Another time, a friend casually offered me a smoke.

He knew I was trying to quit.

When he asked, "What? Did you quit?"—I almost wanted to kick him.

He was still a good friend. But he didn't understand addiction.

And that's not all.

Because friends often remember the old you—the version that was loud, fun, tipsy, casual and more.

And when you quit, they don't know what to do with this calmer, more grounded version of you.

They may now say,

"You used to be more fun."

They don't mean bad at all. But it stings.

And oddly enough, the people who actually respected my choice to quit were strangers.

No pressure. Just respect.

And then, this thought hit me. A powerful one.

Do Olympic gold medalists—like Michael Phelps, Usain Bolt, or Neeraj Chopra—need someone standing by their side every morning saying, "You're the best"?

Do they show off while training, needing applause before the race begins?

No.

They train in silence.

They wake up when the world is still sleeping.

They push themselves beyond pain when no one is watching.

They practice in the dark—for one moment. The Gold.

They don't wait for someone else to call them a champion.

They already know.

They say it to themselves.

That voice that says, *"You're the best"* comes from within.

And maybe that's what we need, too.

Because quitting isn't some public celebration.

It's internal.

A private one.

You might not get applause.

People may not understand you.

You might even be questioned about your anxiety, your restlessness—by people you thought would support you.

So what?

You're not doing this for a medal.

You're doing this for your peace of mind.

To become who you always wanted to be.

That's why you need to say it.

To yourself.

"Well done."

I am proud of my effort, even if no one else sees it.

Let the world not care.

You are not quitting for appreciation.

You are quitting to be real.

Be your own cheerleader.

And that, right there—that's your gold medal.

You're doing it for the version of yourself you've always wanted to be.

Celebrate your small wins, as we discussed—even if no one else does.

Notes:

(Use this space to scribble anything that strikes a chord.
An idea, a plan, or even a feeling.
This space is yours)

Visualise the Future

I'm not talking about visualisation from some spiritual context.

This is a simple execution of imagination, one that makes you feel in the body and mind.

On a lighter note, with reference to the tech world, it's more like using machine learning to train your emotions, feeding it patterns until it knows how to respond on its own.

On a serious note, visualisation is integral to the quitting journey.

It is often ignored simply because you don't get to see results immediately. It all happens in the mind.

It might feel like a figment of imagination.

But the results are real and solid.

Let me tell you how important it really is.

Whether a tall skyscraper or a simple house, it all starts with a blueprint.

A map.

Then comes the foundation—days or weeks building pillars from the underground, preparing for what will stand above.

A structure that won't negotiate with storms and stand firm, rock solid.

It's the same when you're quitting addiction.

You need your blueprint. You need your layout.

You need to see clearly what your life will look like from all sides.

This part of the book connects everything—from that moment you decided, 'Enough is enough. I'm done,' to the point where you finally break free.

So, let's go back to that moment.

Start with the notes you made while being mindful of your thoughts.

What caught your attention?

What were your triggers—internal and external?

You already have a list.

I had one too.

Add every emotional link you had to the substance.

Don't worry if you're still breaking those ties—it's okay.

Ask yourself:

What has to happen for you to lose your ability to quit?

How do you plan to handle the emptiness or void, if any?

Add all of them.

Write them down. Seriously.

It might feel like a huge task, but honestly, it takes just 20 or 25 minutes—maybe 10 more. That's it.

You need not write long sentences. A few words that connect with you on that thing are enough.

Now, say your list adds to 50 points from the whole process.

That's your map.

And silently, your brain is already starting to work on visualising your reactions and responses in future situations as you write them.

Pick each point one by one.

Visualise how you would respond if that trigger, craving, or situation showed up again. Be real, and feel the emotions in your body and mind.

Don't rush this.

Take your time. Spread it across days.

Visualise only what feels real.

I did this repeatedly. And after a while, I didn't even need the list.

It's how the brain rewires itself. That's science, not just an imagination.

I began to see myself breaking free from all that garbage—clearly, vividly.

Bit by bit, without making noise, you're building a life that doesn't need addiction.

This is where your real blueprint to break free begins.

The journey has started.

Now, step back and look at your blueprint, which you're already building.

It is a powerful thing.

Notes:

(Use this space to scribble anything that strikes a chord.
An idea, a plan, or even a feeling.
This space is yours)

Forgiveness and Gratitude

Let me share a few stories—please don't judge the characters until the end. They could be real, someone around us—or within us.

In one home, the youngest brother lived in a joint family of five siblings. They ran a family business. On paper, he was a co-owner. In reality, he was the errand boy. Always available and always helpful. He danced at weddings and helped organise every festival—but deep down, he felt invisible. What started as a drink in hiding became something else over the years—a way to forget pains.

In another house, a teenager had lost his father early. He had loving sisters and a caring mother—a well-educated home. But he longed for someone to look up to—a father figure who just wasn't there. His family pampered him but didn't see the emptiness. That void later found company in cigarettes and alcohol.

Then, there was someone who had always been pampered. He loved comfort more than hard work. Didn't start early in life, didn't save, didn't hustle—because deep down, he always believed someone would bail him out. Usually, his father. But his father was tough on him and thought he was weak.

Criticised him. Substances slowly became his escape—first from judgment, then from himself.

Different stories. Different places.

Same outcome.

Each of them felt wronged by life in their own way.

And with that came anger. Shame. Guilt. Loneliness.

They all felt like victims. And when you feel like a victim long enough, it becomes easy to say:

"I deserve this drink. This smoke. This escape."

And, One good day, they decide to quit.

But the old memories—the reasons they started—kept coming back.

And they relapsed.

So, what could break that connection with old memories?

While we discussed this earlier in cutting the emotional chords, here is more about it.

Forgiveness.

The younger brother in the joint family.

The teenager missing his father.

The man who was always criticised.

They could have forgiven the people and situations that made them feel small, resentful, and unworthy.

But if forgiving others was all it took, we would be healed by now.

We forgive people who hurt us. Demeaned us. Abused their dominance.

But we still carry the resentment.

Why?

Two reasons:

We haven't forgiven ourselves.

We've missed being grateful for what we have.

Let's talk about the first one: **forgiving ourselves.**

Forgive ourselves? For what?

Maybe for—

Letting others act the way they did.

Hurting others. Being selfish.

Being weak.

Living in delusion—thinking our pain was bigger than the pain we caused.

Hearts we broke.

Trust we shattered.

Opportunities we wasted.

And for every time we screwed up, telling ourselves we didn't know better, when we actually did.

Whatever else you need to forgive yourself for—**say it.**

This isn't just about karma—it's neuroscience.

How do we forgive ourselves?

That's the hard part.

It requires real regret.

It requires real grief.

And the courage to sit silently with that thought without making excuses.

Asking yourself honestly:

"What will I do differently now?"

That's where self-forgiveness begins.

Not by forgetting.

Not by excusing.

But by accepting yourself—flaws, past, everything.

Love yourself.

Say that loud to yourself, again and again.

Unconditionally.

Some people say that some 50000 thoughts cross our mind daily, sounds unbelievable, but if true add another five about forgiving yourself and gratitude.

Because, Forgiveness and gratitude are a combo—they rarely come alone.

We can't completely forgive while still living with resentment.

And resentment doesn't leave until we start being grateful for what we have.

You know, there could be an entire book written about gratitude.

It makes us human.

It means seeing the good things you once missed.

It could be about simple as being able to breathe, see, eat, or even wake up in the morning.

When you begin to feel grateful, you don't just heal—**you build strength**.

The kind that helps you stay free.

Grateful that you never gave up.

Grateful that you chose to break free.

Notes:

(Use this space to scribble anything that strikes a chord.
An idea, a plan, or even a feeling.
This space is yours)

Disrupt Your Own Narrative About Addictions

A father was talking to his grown up son, who was leaving home for a random job abroad.

The parents had been hoping he might finally get serious about life once he moved away from his useless friends.

Before he left, the father said:

"Just make sure you don't find the same kind of company there, too—we're too old now to worry about you."

The son stood there, mixed up in his thoughts.

He was stepping into a new world with no friends, nothing, but a part of him felt happy—finally, he was getting away from the sarcasm and criticism at home.

Both of them, the father and the son - were carrying a narrative about each other.

It wasn't just an opinion.

Narratives are deeper.

They are the whole stories we keep telling ourselves without even realising it.

The parents' narrative might change once they see their son in good company and doing well.

The son's narrative might change, too—maybe only when he becomes a father one day and feels that same helplessness watching his child make wrong decisions.

Now, imagine if the son's old friends weren't people—but addictions.

Alcohol. Tobacco.

He's in a new country now. A new beginning without that company.

But unless he disrupts his old narrative about addictions—unless he sees them for what they really are—he will carry the same habits with him.

And the same old stories.

And, to disrupt something, you first need to know what you're disrupting.

The old narrative.

Let me share what mine were—which I only realised after quitting:

Old – "I can quit anytime."

Disrupt – How long had I been living in that delusion?

Old – "I just take a little."

Disrupt – Then why did I end up where I was?

Old – "It helps me focus."

Disrupt – Then why did I lose even the little focus I had left?

Old – "It's my way to unwind."

Disrupt – Did you feel that way, really?

Old – "I am not addicted."

Disrupt – So who is? Who defines it? Me? Say that again after you quit.

Who made old narratives?

Me? When? After addiction?

Wow.

But with that disruption, I realised something:

Every old story ends the moment you stop narrating it.

So before disrupting the narrative, I asked myself,

Is it helping me?

Maybe I can change the script. The pen is in my hand.

Isn't it.

Notes:

(Use this space to scribble anything that strikes a chord.
An idea, a plan, or even a feeling.
This space is yours)

Let the New Narrative Sink In

Now, you have a new narrative about addiction, alcohol or tobacco.

Potentially powerful and a real one.

But it could still be building up. Still settling.

And the truth is that many people around could carry a narrative of convenience.

At times, they come with distorted wisdom about addiction.

With a stupid rationale like 'Rum is good for winters' or 'beer is not alcohol'

You'll hear it all.

So, what's my point here?

Stay clear of such people—at least for now.

I did that. It helped. Believe me.

I once tried sharing the science of quitting with a friend—a chain smoker.

Didn't go well. I got unfriended.

Not just from Facebook—But from real life.

Let me digress.

I recall a story where there were two friends.

One had a crore in the bank.

The other had just one lakh.

Both friends tried to convince each other that they were happier with the money they had in the bank.

The friend with One Lac said

"Two hundred rupees is all I need to eat in a day.

Every extra rupee does not add value to me. I am so happy I don't have money, which doesn't add value."

The other friend with 100 times more money just walked away, confused and probably.,

That is how convincing people sound with their distorted opinion about addictions.

So—let the new narrative sink in.

Because later—maybe after a few months—

You won't have to say anything to prove how it feels to break free from the addictions.

You will *be the* proof.

Oh, and while we are still talking about it,

Let me add a superstition angle.

"Working quietly protects from the evil eye—especially the ones that secretly want you to stay addicted."

Well, that was a joke.

Or maybe not. You decide.

Let the world keep its opinions.

Let your life do the talking—soon enough.

Notes:

(Use this space to scribble anything that strikes a chord.
An idea, a plan, or even a feeling.
This space is yours)

When you are ready, it's your turn.

I don't know if you are ready to quit now and break free from addictions.

And it's okay if you still need another hour, a day, a month, or even more.

But when you find yourself saying, "Enough. I'm done with it,"

trust that you're already stronger than you think.

Maybe that moment is now.

And if you haven't reached that point yet, that's okay too.

You are already closer than you were yesterday.

Because for some, change doesn't need a dramatic moment.

Sometimes, it simply begins inside you, quietly, in your own way.

I have made a workbook; honestly, it's not a manual.

It's just a Churaiya.

If you don't remember the Churaiya reference from earlier in the book—let me share it again:

In kite flying, when someone is new or finds it difficult, they ask a friend to help.

The friend stands a bit farther away, holding the kite tied with the thread.

You hold the thread.

And when you're ready, the friend sets the kite free—

hurling it toward the sky.

And the kite flies because **you** have the control now.

This book and the workbook are like that friend.

A small support, so you can fly. Break free.

I would be most happy to hear your success story someday.

And who knows, maybe I will get to learn something from you too.

Until then. I look forward to it.

Bipin Gupta

A Friend

References

https://www.who.int/news-room/fact-sheets/detail/tobacco

https://www.who.int/news/item/25-06-2024-over-3-million-annual-deaths-due-to-alcohol-and-drug-use-majority-among-men

https://www.imdb.com/title/tt0120382/   Truman show

https://www.imdb.com/title/tt0343660/   Fifty first dates

https://www.phrases.org.uk/meanings/a-rose-is-a-rose-is-a-rose.html

https://pubmed.ncbi.nlm.nih.gov/29169665/

https://jamanetwork.com/journals/jamapsychiatry/fullarticle/1839290?utm_source=chatgpt.com

https://www.alzheimers.net/11-3-14-dementia-food-cravings?

Part Four

Workbook

Welcome

So, here you are—with me.

How has the journey been so far as you moved through this book?

I believe some parts may have really resonated with you, while others might not have hit home as much—and that's completely okay. We're all unique.

But you know what? Even doctors often prescribe the same medicine to two people with the same diagnosis—yet each person responds differently.

That's something we might share.

I'm not a doctor, but I'm here to share what's worked for me—insights, tools, and questions that guided me on this path.

The purpose of this workbook is to be a support as you work toward breaking free. While I may not be right there with you, I hope these pages serve as a steady, rock solid support on your journey.

And now, it's time to make this workbook truly your own.

Here you go…

How This Workbook Is Structured

To make things easy and useful, I have divided this workbook into three parts:

***Part 1** is about gentle reflection on the chapters from the main book. It aims to help you **DIG DEEPER**—in your own tone and language. Say what feels true. Write what works best for you.*

***Part 2** includes daily reflection lists drawn directly from my personal practice—the thoughts and reminders that helped me break free.*

I have also added simple guidance on how to use these lists, so you can make the most of them.

***Part 3** is something to read just in case you ever slip back. Think of it as an emergency read, like a friendly voice telling you,*

"Someone is there for you."

Workbook Part 1

Dig Deeper

This part is about finding your moment of truth. Being real.

Not fixing anything.

Just feel what's really going on and put it into words.

These questions aren't about perfection—they are just about reflection, awareness, honesty, and moving on.

You still own it.

You still lead yourself.

And this is how you break free.

We all do.

My reasons to quit, which I only know and hate to say

Dig Deeper

How does it really feel when you think about those reasons—the ones you hate to say out loud?

(Don't filter it. What happens in your body when you think about them?)

What makes quitting more important than anything else right now?

(This could be even beyond your real 'WHY'.)

How do you imagine yourself once you've addressed those WHYs and moved past them?

(Describe it like you already made it there.)

What's the difference between the reasons that sound right and the ones that hit hard? Very hard?

(What is the real monster, WHY, the one that made you say Enough, I am done?)

What would it be like if you had to pass on what you learned about 'why quit addictions' in just a few words—a one-liner?

(Make it yours. Something that can motivate the generations to come.)

I am a fighter and just not afraid of falling down.

Dig deeper

What does "falling down" really mean to *you*, in your own story?

(Go beyond the word. Write the feeling, the moment, the meaning.)

Recall a moment when you surprised yourself by getting back up stronger? What helped you?

(Dig into the turning point, however small.)

If you slipped, what would *not* help? And what would?

(Be brutally honest)

What is that hidden courage in you that people never got to see?

(Name it. Now is the time)

Write a one-liner that you would tell someone who almost made it but pulled back at the last moment—a boxer who could have won the championship but chose not to.

Vulnerability is my strength.
I respect that.

Dig Deeper

How does it really feel when you ask someone close for help, and they don't show up for some reason?

(Go there. What does it feel like in your body, your heart?)

What would you do if you needed support and only had one person to count on—someone you don't even get along with?

(Would you still ask? Or take the risk and go solo?)

Can you ask or even demand help when it matters the most?

(Be honest. What stops you? What lets you?)

When you visit a doctor when you're unwell, do you feel like asking for help or just doing what's needed?

(And why would emotional support feel any different?)

Write a one-liner you'd say to someone who just needs to ask for support to change their life.

(Say it like you mean it.)

My thoughts can't escape the radar.

Dig deeper.

How do you think we can become more mindful of our thoughts?

(What works? What doesn't? What would it take for you?)

What would change if we were more mindful of our thoughts and emotions?

(Say it from your experience)

■ Enough I am done with it ■

Recall a time when you were angry, really angry.

(Were you aware of it as it happened, or did the awareness come later?)

How does being mindful of your thoughts—even the hidden ones—make you a different kind of person?

(Name it. Own it.)

Write a one-liner you'd say to someone who speaks out, whatever comes to mind, with no filter.

(Say it straight.)

I can handle triggers.

Dig Deeper

What are your biggest triggers that have always led you back?

(Be specific. People, places, moods, timings—name them.)

Imagine you've quit and stayed clean for a whole month.
What needs to happen for a craving to comeback?
(Be real with it. This helps.)

If you were on a different planet where that substance didn't exist, what would help you the most when cravings hit?

(Reflect)

What makes you believe that you can handle the cravings better this time?

(Be honest. What's different now?

Write a one-liner for someone who thinks cravings are the most challenging part of breaking free.

(Write like it could shake them up.)

I accept myself the way I am

Dig Deeper

What does it really take to accept yourself, including the flaws, the past, and the mess?

(No sugarcoating.)

How does self-acceptance help when you're trying to change something as deep as addiction?

(What changes)

When you accept yourself with flaws, does it mean you are accepting flaws?

(Reflect - what's the difference between accepting and justifying?)

Write a one-liner you would say to someone who is waiting to be perfect before they can love themselves.

(Say it from your gut.)

I am grateful

Dig Deeper

Is being grateful an emotion or a state of mind to you? How would you explain that, if you had to?

(Reflect from the experiences)

Can we be grateful for our wrong choices?

(Do they leave you with learnings and new perspectives)

How does gratitude feel in your body when you actually mean it, not just say it?

(Slow down. Feel it. Say it.)

Write a one-liner you would tell someone who says, "There's nothing to be grateful for."

(How would you make them see the reality)

Forgiveness

Dig deeper

What's the most challenging part about forgiving yourself for past blunders or mistakes?

(And how could you start handling that—even in small ways?)

What emotions would come up if you actually forgave yourself?

(Imagine it actually happened.)

What emotions would you feel if you forgave someone else for their past mistakes?

(Write honestly, even if it takes time.)

What could stop you from forgiving yourself or others?

(This is where the resistance lives.)

Do we have to be vocal when asking for forgiveness from someone we've hurt?

(What if we can't or are not ready to be?)

Workbook Part 2

The Author's Personal Daily List - 1 (First 30 Days)

What is this list —

I sat down to compile the thoughts, reflections, and inner strengths that helped me quit addictions. Here are my most helpful top 20.

I have framed them as honest reflections for your self-rating.

I encourage you to spend ten minutes daily on the List.

Circle, score, scribble, or just sit with them. Let them be your transparent reflections, your silent support.

Also, I don't know what you want to quit, Alcohol, cigarettes or gutkha, so to make it easier, I have referred to it as 'Addiction.'

Before you go to the List

This isn't just a checklist. These statements were thoughtfully crafted with care to give you a gentle reminder of the journey you have just started.

Quitting an addiction can be hard, but staying free takes something deeper.

It asks you to rebuild from within—your emotions, beliefs, habits, and sense of self.

These reflections are here to help you stay steady, grounded, honest, and emotionally aware.

(Self-rating is out of 10 for how much you resonate with each statement.

If you score less than 10, take a moment to breathe. Recall your WHY list or the strength you felt when you first made the choice to change or said, 'Enough, I am done with it.'

Each effort compounds like cumulative returns—every positive choice brings you closer to breaking free. You just need to make that 100%.)

1. ***I am completely committed to taking ownership and being responsible for TODAY to go without addiction.***

   a. 10   b. Less than 10

2. ***No one is coming to save me or appreciate for quitting it. This is my life, my choice.***

   a. 10   b. Less than 10

3. ***My WHY list gives me the same resolve and determination as it did when I first wrote it.***

   a. 10   b. Less than 10

4. *I know exactly why I want to quit. And it is embedded in my awareness.*

   a. 10   b. Less than 10

5. *I know that I was not born with any addictions and can for sure feel the same way now. Same emotions, same me.*

   a. 10   b. Less than 10

6. *Even if I have a weak moment, I will still stick to my decision to quit.*

   a. 10   b. Less than 10

7. *I am open to learn, ask for help and support in my journey to break free from addictions.*

   a. 10   b. Less than 10

8. *My complete focus is to stay clean of any addiction today.*

   a. 10   b. Less than 10

9. *I am completely aware of my triggers and actively avoid them to protect my recovery.*

   a. 10   b. Less than 10

10. *I am mentally prepared with responses when someone offers me what I have quit.*

    a. 10   b. Less than 10

11. *I have more strategies to handle pressure when someone offers me what I have quit.*

    a. 10   b. Less than 10

12. *I believe I can handle cravings and triggers confidently, even during vulnerable moments.*

    a. 10   b. Less than 10

13. *I proactively revisit my WHY list, even on calm days, to stay grounded in my purpose.*

    a. 10   b. Less than 10

14. *I remind myself daily that my peace of mind is more important than the pleasure which addiction gave to me.*

    a. 10   b. Less than 10

15. *I am clear that there could be moments of boredom, but I am prepared to handle them in my own way and have plans that support me in my journey.*

    a. 10   b. Less than 10

16. *I feel proud of the effort I am making, even if no one else appreciates or notices.*

    a. 10   b. Less than 10

17. *I strongly believe this will make me a better version of myself. Someone, I deeply respect.*

    a. 10   b. Less than 10

18. *I know withdrawal symptoms may show up like anxiety or restlessness. And I am ready to handle them with strength and awareness.*

    a. 10   b. Less than 10

19. *I know that seeking medical supervision is important when quitting addictions.*

    a. 10   b. Less than 10

20. *I am aware that fear may show up, fear of failing, cravings, or not making it. But I trust myself to move through it with courage and strength.*

    a. 10   b. Less than 10

The Author's Personal Daily List - 2

To keep it simple, I have shared two lists. The earlier one is for your first 30 days, but honestly, that list is helpful any day.

This second list is for when you've crossed the early hurdles.

Let me honestly congratulate you on that—it's a stellar achievement. Believe me, the most difficult part is behind you.

This stage could feel like a tightrope walker who's made it a quarter of the way—still focused, still steady—knowing it's not over until the other side is reached.

But in addiction recovery, there's no fixed destination, just as staying healthy is not a one-time achievement.

It's a journey.

So, while you would follow this list, some days you'll return to List 1, and some days both.

They are reflections that I found indispensable.

(Self-rating is out of 10 for how much you resonate with each statement.

If you score less than 10, take a moment to breathe. Recall your WHY list or the strength you felt when you first made the choice to change or said, 'Enough, I am done with it.'

Each effort compounds like cumulative returns—every positive choice brings you closer to breaking free. You just need to make that 100%.)

1. **I have started to feel like the person I was before addictions—like that's who I really am.**

   a. 10

   b. Less than 10

2. **I fully accept myself—who I was, and who I am becoming. I love myself completely.**

   a. 10

   b. Less than 10

3. **My values around health, happiness, and peace are very clear, and they give me strength to stay out of addictions.**

   a. 10

   a. Less than 10

4. **I understand that relapse can happen. If it does, I won't be angry at myself or feel let down – I will reflect and start again. I would have learned something for sure.**

   a. 10

   b. Less than 10

5. *I'm deeply grateful for all I have—and surprised by how long my gratitude list has become. I'm thankful for everything, every day.*

   a.   *10*

   b.   *Less than 10*

6. *Even the pain and challenges after quitting have made me wiser. They've grounded me to see things clearly about addictions.*

   a.   *10*

   b.   *Less than 10*

7. *I am aware of the risks, like overconfidence or complacency, and I stay connected to my WHY and inner self daily.*

   a.   *10*

   b.   *Less than 10*

8. *I do realise that some parts of my past might still need forgiveness, especially from myself, and I forgive myself with a promise not to repeat them.*

   a.   *10*

   b.   *Less than 10*

9. *I can feel that cravings and triggers are losing their power over me.*

   a.   *10*

   b.   *Less than 10*

10. *I allow myself to feel all emotions, including uncertainty, without judgment.*

    a. *10*

    b. *Less than 10*

11. *When I feel restless or unsettled, I listen inwardly, try to understand what needs attention, and work on it.*

    a. *10*

    b. *Less than 10*

12. *I eat meals on time and drink a lot of water.*

    a. *10*

    b. *Less than 10*

13. *I intentionally include something that gives me joy, such as moments of creativity or spending time with loved ones, even if it's small.*

    a. *10*

    b. *Less than 10*

14. *After every clean day, I see how beautiful an addiction-free life is.*

    a. *10*

    b. *Less than 10*

15. *I have started to understand that quitting is not just a goal—it's a new way of living I choose every day.*

    a.   10

    b.   Less than 10

16. *I no longer carry illusions about addiction—I see it for what it truly is.*

    a.   10

    b.   Less than 10

17. *I feel pride in caring for my body, mind, and soul—it reflects how I show up for life.*

    a.   10

    b.   Less than 10

18. *I forgive the people who hurt me, knowingly or unknowingly, from my heart. Maybe they did what felt right to them then. My resentment is fading because I'm choosing what's right for me. And I am thankful for what I have.*

    a.   10

    b.   Less than 10

19. *I don't judge people when I see them with addictions.*

    a.   10

    b.   Less than 10

Workbook part 3

Break the Glass in Case of Emergency

(When you might have slipped back and need to rise again.)

In the buildings, there is always that small glass window red box with some tool inside.

It says: Break in case of emergency.

Often, we never had to break it as there was never an emergency.

But just knowing it's there gives us comfort.

A belief that if something goes wrong, there is something to lean on.

This chapter is your red box.

It was already here before you needed it.

And now that you're here, let me tell you something with complete honesty:

You are still doing great.

I am not a doctor.

But I am certainly someone who has been through this myself.

And the first time I slipped?

I felt confusion, guilt, shame and even anger.

I slipped because, I felt a craving for the old version of me. The addicted version.

That familiar "high" I once thought was my comfort.

Maybe I felt that change is difficult and painful.

But after slipping back, I experienced something unexpected.

I didn't enjoy that addiction anymore.

It was like being in a relationship you know is wrong.

I had a gut feeling, a strong intuition:

How could I lose my goal so easily?

And with my normal instinct -

I googled it.

The Moment I Googled: "Is relapsing part of recovery?"

I found something comforting. Insightful. Helpful.

Relapse is actually part of recovery.

And not just one opinion—hundreds of articles, studies, and lived experiences confirm it.

So, here's what I believe now:

It is not a failure.

It is not the end.

It is part of the process.

It means something inside me still needs healing.

That's it.

Nothing more. Nothing less.

Because my reset button was still intact.

I could choose to RISE back to my journey.

And I did.

What Helped Me Stand Up Again?

I opened my WHY list—and added more.

I added this line:

"I relapsed because I needed to heal more. And now I know better—I'm stronger."

Surprisingly, I felt more grounded after returning to recovery.

Triggers were dying.

I wasn't scared of the craving anymore, because I got up again after slipping.

Let's Talk About You

Take five minutes.

Google whatever you want about relapse or slipping.

Take some time to reflect.

You can get up again if you have not done so yet.

100%.

Maybe write this down—honestly, without judgment:

- What did I feel right before the relapse?

- What do I know better now?

- What helped to make a comeback?

One Last Thing

Nobody comes this far to give up.

And you are still walking forward, even if this chapter is the pause you needed.